ON FIRE

ALSO BY LARRY BROWN

Facing the Music

stories

Dirty Work

a novel

Big Bad Love

stories

Joe

a novel

LARRY BROWN

ON FIRE

ALGONQUIN BOOKS OF CHAPEL HILL

1994

Published by

Algonquin Books of Chapel Hill

Post Office Box 2225

Chapel Hill, North Carolina 27515-2225

a division of

Workman Publishing Company, Inc.

708 Broadway

New York, New York 10003

Printed in the United States of America

Design by Molly Renda

Excerpts from *On Fire* first appeared in *The North American Review*. Sections of an early manuscript version of it appeared in *The Oxford American.*

Library of Congress Cataloging-in-Publication Data

Brown, Larry, 1951 July 9–

On fire / Larry Brown.—1st ed.

p. cm.

ISBN 1-56512-009-4

1. Brown, Larry, 1951 July 9– 2. Fire fighters—United States—Biography. I. Title.

TH9118.B76A3 1994

363.37'092—dc20

[B] 93-26094 CIP

First Edition

10 9 8 7 6 5 4 3 2 1

This book is for Sam: faithful friend, loyal companion.

AUTHOR'S NOTE

I joined the Oxford, Mississippi, Fire Department when I was 22. It was a big step up for me after driving trucks and forklifts, and I didn't figure back in 1973 that I'd ever do anything but spend the next thirty years fighting fires.

But a man never knows what's going to become of his life. We aren't given any promises that we'll even live through childhood, that we won't have to go to war, that we won't end up dead in a car on some highway.

Writing was a curveball that I never saw coming. It's such an improbable and foolish-sounding thing to say in front of anybody: "I'm going to become a writer. I'm going to learn how to write a book." But I did tell that to a good friend of mine one day a little over twelve years ago, up in a pasture near a pond we were fishing in, and he didn't laugh. He might have found it hard to believe that I could accomplish such a thing, but he didn't laugh. He just listened to me seriously and nodded his head.

I figured writing might be like learning how to build houses or lay brick, or even fight fires. I had one burning thought that I believed was true. If I wrote long enough and hard enough, I'd eventually learn how. My only obligation was feeding my family while I was trying to learn how to do this other thing, and that meant to keep working at the fire department plus the usual extra stuff like carrying bricks and mixing mortar and swinging a hammer and cutting pulpwood with a chain saw. But I was willing to do all that in order to have the scattered afternoons and weekends to write. From 1980 on I wrote steadily, filling up pages, mailing off manuscripts, publishing a story every couple of years and then finally a first book of stories in 1988. There've been two novels and another book of stories since then.

I left the fire department over three years ago, and it's been over four since I started writing *On Fire*. An autobiographical book like this is something new for me. Up to now it's just been stories and poems and novels. It's all just stories, no matter how long they are or what form they take. And any book in progress is kind of like a friend who comes and stays with you for a good long while, who lives in the house and inside your mind. It stays there through meals and sleeping and waking and cutting the grass and tending to the kids and taking out the garbage. When the book is being formed in your mind and on the page, I mean the actual accumulation of the work itself, day by day or hour by hour, it has a life of its own and it is living for that period of time with you.

All that was true with *On Fire*. But certain things were different this time around. I'd spent years imagining things for my fiction, all the stories and the novels I'd written. In this case, however, every event had already happened—or was happening as I wrote it, when I was still at the fire department. Usually it was a simple matter of remembering the situations, and that wasn't hard because so many of the things that happened over those sixteen years left an indelible impression on my memory. You don't forget death and pain, or fear. All the events were there, but I had to try and make some sense out of it.

This book is an attempt to explore what I felt about my years in the fire service and what it was like to live through those years, and the way two totally different careers had to mesh and make room for each other, until one of them finished first. There's a ton of stuff that's not in here that could've been, but in whatever I'm writing, I want to put in only the things the story needs and leave everything else out. I've tried to do that here as well.

Larry Brown
May 26, 1993
Yocona, Mississippi

I love what I do with my hands and with the hose. I love the knots I know how to tie, the clove hitch for raising equipment to a high window, the mighty bowline that is the only one you can trust your life to, the only one you tie before rappelling off a building. You tie it to a chimney or a strong piece of steel and then you run the line through the steel loop at your safety belt and then you step off the edge and lean back and trust your life to it, and it never lets you down. You walk backwards down the side of the building, not ever fearing, not ever thinking about what might happen if it slips, because it won't slip. You have to believe in the bowline before you can believe you can rappel.

I love the way the lights are set up on the side of the road at a wreck and I love the way the Hurst Tool opens with its incredible strength and I love the way it crushes the roof posts of a car and I love the way you can nudge it into the hinges of a door and pop the pins off and let the door fall and reach in to see your patient's legs and what position they are in.

I love to drive to any incident, love to run the siren, to run fast but careful through town. I love the smell of smoke and the feeling of fear that comes on me when I see that a fire is already through the roof and licking at the sky because I know that I am about to be tested again, my muscles, my brain, my heart.

I love my old torn-up boots, the toes skinned and burned, my wrinkled gloves, sootstreaked and charred, my dirty coat and frayed turnout pants.

I love to go down on the floor and see the smoke over me, worm my way forward to the fire, the hose as hard as a brick, the scuffed rubber on the end of the fog nozzle. I love the two-and-a-half-inch hoses and the big chrome nozzles that no one man can hold, the red axes and the pry bars and the pike poles that we tear down ceilings with, looking for devious pockets of fire, sneaky little bastards that will smolder and rekindle the house after we're back at the fire station asleep in our beds, and I love to stand at the pump panel and set the relief valve and hear it open when a line is shut down, and I love to know that I can operate this $200,000 piece of equipment like I've been taught so that nobody will get his ass burned up because of me. I love going to a bar called Ireland's with my partners when we're off duty, and I love the movies we watch at the station and the meals we cook and eat and the targets we shoot with our bows in the afternoons, washing our cars and trucks in the parking lot and sitting out front of the station in chairs at night hollering at people we know passing on the street. These men are like a family to me, and the only thing I can relate it to is being in the Marine Corps, where everybody, black or white or brown or tan, wore the same uniform, all assembled for a common purpose, a brotherhood. This thing's the same thing.

I'm a grown man but I only weigh about 135 pounds soaking wet. I'm nearly the smallest guy in the department, which is a disadvantage sometimes when feats of strength are called for. Say, if you're breaking down a door with an ax beside some big guy who is about six foot three and 250 or so. All you can do is keep swinging, keep trying to get the job done.

Our department has thirty-nine men, three stations, four pumpers, one ladder truck that will also pump plenty, one crash truck, one van, three pickups, and two cars and three miles of hose. We also have ladders, axes, forcible entry tools, rappelling gear, ropes, safety belts, breathing apparatus, nozzles, generators, a Hurst Tool (Jaws of Life), flashlights, pike poles, entry saws, boltcutters, fire extinguishers, and many many many other tools.

All of this stuff is very expensive and most of it will hurt you, pinch your fingers off, cut you or bruise you or abrade you in some way that will be pretty painful later. I say later because of adrenaline. Your kid knocks the car out of gear, it begins to roll down a hill, you run and catch it and stop it by grabbing the bumper because of adrenaline. A man turns a tractor over on himself, and his son lifts it off. That, too, is adrenaline at work, the gland flowing, making you more than you normally would be. The adrenaline starts pumping when we run to the trucks. When the big starter kicks in and she rolls over and coughs like a dinosaur waking up, the adrenaline is flowing. It makes you not feel pain, not ignore it, actually, just *not even feel it* when it happens. It's happened to me and I've seen it happen to other men at fires and wrecks, and it's there to protect you, make you strong so you don't get hurt. Adrenaline lets people do what they have to, what they might not be able to do without it even if they had to.

Potential disaster: maybe that's why I can't sleep. I fear two things more than others: a leaking gasoline tanker and a leaking liquid propane container, whether stationary or on wheels, turned over in a ditch or whatever. Ignition, from whatever source, a cigarette, the hot tailpipe or manifold on a car down the road, will be what kills you and all your men, your pretty red fire trucks, anybody else who couldn't or didn't run. But I also fear ammonium nitrate, and Malathion, and planes crashing at my airport, and lots of other things. Wrecks on the way to anything. Backdrafts, flashovers. Also not having anything decent on HBO to watch when I'm on duty. We prefer S and V (sex and violence), but we'll go with a nature show on The Discovery Channel if that's all that's flowing. We can't stay adrenalined up all the time.

Things in this room: Radio. Mike. Scanner. Encoder. Fire phone. Dispatcher's desk. Chair. *Playboy* magazines. Maps. A five-foot-square aerial photo of the University of Mississippi. TV. VCR. Uniform shirts hanging on the wall. Microwave. Stove. Refrigerator. Sink. Coffee pot. An empty cake bell smeared with pink frosting. A four-foot stick with a crooked plastic finger screwed into the end of it with the ominous words THE FINGER written on it in green ink. Shoeshine kit. A table and some captain's chairs. Photographs of us in action. Two folded flags, one United States, one Mississippi. Liquid Paper. Playing cards. Hundreds of telephone numbers. Run reports. A PA system. A flyswatter. A digital clock flashing 5:51. Some tomatoes. An onion. A cantaloupe. Keys. A videocassette of *Top Gun*. Yesterday's newspapers. Day before yesterday's newspapers. Memos from Uncle Chiefy. Coffee cups. Somebody's dirty socks. A whetrock. Ink pens. Cartoons about firemen.

Now I'm sleepy, with fifty-five minutes to go before I get off duty. My partners have been moaning and groaning back there in the bedroom with the pre-wake jitters. I'm the world's worst about talking in my sleep. They can and do carry on conversations with me while I'm conked out. I've been known to talk about John Wayne, or just holler out something crazy and wake myself up. I think I must have a sleeping disorder, but I don't think I need to go to the doctor about it. I think I only have it when I'm up here. When I'm home in my own bed with Mary Annie, I sleep fine. I don't have a fire phone in my bedroom.

I think all these things are connected, adrenaline and sleep and Mary Annie and fear and THE FINGER and a bunch of guys piled up in beds snoring in the dark.

I just stepped outside to get the paper, just as the garbage-men rode by. I waved, they waved. Their work day is just beginning. Mine will be over in forty-five minutes if the fire phone doesn't ring. I hope it doesn't ring. I'll be happy to stay right here and read or write and watch movies and eat. Maybe even sleep some. It sure would be nice.

Fear. The fine line you walk where what you have to do drives you to do it up against what your better judgment tells you not to. A firefighter cannot be a coward. He can be a lot of things, a prick, a thief, a liar, but he cannot be a coward and he probably will not be a child molester, although I'd bet somebody a million dollars there is at least one child molester somewhere in the fire service. A man who won't tote his own weight, who won't hump his own hose, won't be tolerated. They'll blackball him and nobody will want him on his shift. I've seen men who were reluctant to enter a burning building. It does not endear them to you, not if you think about going down inside one and him being the only one immediately available to pull you out. But there's not anybody I'm working with that I'm uneasy about. This is as it should be. Our biggest worry most days is what to eat and what to watch on HBO. This is as it should be, too. Our motto is, A well-rested firefighter is a good firefighter.

Potential disaster was averted a while ago, around two-thirty. I was back there, trying to go to sleep but actually just rolling around in the dark, and the fire phone rang. There was a gas main leaking on Jackson Avenue, and a large amount of gas had apparently already escaped, so everything we have went out the door except for the ladder truck and the crash truck.

These sleepyheads had it all under control when I arrived in the van and went 10-23. That means you're on the scene, engaged in an assignment. Our crew was catching a plug and had already advanced an inch-and-a-half hand line down the street and put the nozzle in a fog pattern to disperse the gas. Standard procedure. Evidently some dilbert-headed gal or guy had come out of a bar called Forrester's with one too many cold ones under his or her belt, backed over the gas main, and then driven off without telling anybody about it. Bad move. A police officer just happened to be driving by a block away and smelled it.

If, at close range, you've never heard a three-quarter-inch gas main shrieking all its gas out at once, you'd probably be pretty surprised at how loud it is. Somebody has to go right up to it while they hold a fog stream on it and try to get a plug down inside the pipe and stop the leak. Johnny was already doing that when I walked up. I got down next to him and held a flashlight for him. The water ran down inside my turnout coat and started getting my shirt and cigarettes wet. We used to use things the boys called butt plugs, conical hard rubber plugs you drove down into the pipe with a hammer. Now we have rubberized expanding plugs with a long shank that you insert deep into the pipe and then turn with a wing nut until it seals. You don't want to get one down in there and not get it tight enough. It'll fly back out like a bullet and knock your eyeball out. All this is happening while you're bent over, wondering if the gas has spread out enough to find an ignition source. It's nervous-making, but duty you have to do.

It worked. We sealed the leak, called the gas company, and nothing was ignited. It just smelled like a two-thousand-ton fart. We rolled the hose up and went back home. Then I went to bed and rolled around in the dark for a long time and then finally decided that since I couldn't sleep, I might as well get up and write. Plus, the snoring was driving me crazy.

I was cooking some ribs one evening and drinking a beer, taking life easy on a Saturday afternoon. The ribs were parboiling in some water, getting tender, and about dark I was going to put them over a fire on the grill, slap some barbecue sauce on them, cook my family a little feast. Maybe we were going to watch a movie, too, I don't know. That's one of our big things: cook something on the grill outside and then watch a good movie while we're eating, then kind of just fall out all over the living room to finish watching it, then sometimes even watch another one. I usually have several cold beers while I'm doing that. The ribs were going to cook for a couple of hours and I had plenty of beer.

The phone rang and my plans got changed. It was the dispatcher at Station No. 1, and he said we had a fire at the

Law School at Ole Miss, and all hands were being called in. It was what we call a Code Red.

I cut off the ribs but I did take my beer. I thought if the fire wasn't too bad, a beer would be pretty good on the way back. I drove my little truck at what is an abnormal speed for me, about sixty-five. I live about ten miles from Oxford so it didn't take long to get there.

You never know what to expect except that if it's bad you can certainly expect to be dirty and exhausted and possibly coughing or throwing up or maybe even burned, your ears singed a little before it's over. I knew the building but I'd only been in the bottom of it once, and in the library once, and that was on the second floor. The fire we had that night was on the fifth, top floor.

I stopped by Station No. 1 and got my turnouts, pulling my pickup right into the truck bay where a lot of leather boots were lying, where my partners had kicked them off and left them. The turnout pants stand on low shelves, folded down with the rubber boots already inside them, so that all you have to do is step into them and pull the pants up, snap them shut, grab your coat and helmet, climb on the truck and roll out the door. Every piece of equipment in the house was gone, our big diesel pumper, the van, and the ladder truck that could reach ten stories high. The dispatcher came out for a second and said we had a working fire but they didn't know how bad it was yet. I drove fast through town, knowing where all the cops were.

The ladder truck was being set up when I pulled into the parking lot. There was a little smoke showing from the top of the building. I could see our boys in full gear down on their knees putting airpacks on. I put my turnouts on, got my gloves in one hand and my helmet in the other, and ran to report to the assistant chief in charge that I was there and ready for my assignment. Off-duty people were arriving all around me. They'd called everybody in.

The structure was a five-story building with a concrete exterior, lined with windows about seven or eight feet long and about five and a half feet tall. None of the windows were designed to open, had no hinges or handles, and the glass was tempered, somewhere between a quarter and a half inch thick. There was no outside egress to the building except through the first and top floors. It was not equipped with a sprinkler system, since it was considered to be a fireproof building, but it did have a wet standpipe system with those little piss-ant hoses.

I found out that the alarm inside the building had been going for quite a while, but people had simply ignored it. Kept walking around in there, conducting their whatever. I was told to put on an airpack and climb the stairwell with some other firefighters to the top floor and descend into the building to try and locate the fire. I donned my apparatus, found my partners, and we started up. We all had flashlights.

The rig weighs between thirty and forty pounds. It will give you about twenty minutes of air if you're lying flat on your back breathing through the respirator; that's if you're not exerting yourself. When five minutes of air is left, a little bell mounted on the tank will start ringing, loud and insistently, driven by the declining air pressure. With experience you learn to leave the mask off until you're ready to enter your dangerous atmosphere. They work just like a diver's rig, but the mask and mouthpiece are all molded together, so that the mask covers your whole face. They're called SCBA, self-contained breathing apparatus. You can enter a poisonous atmosphere, live in a superheated temperature if the rest of your body can stand it. The main purpose is to prevent the firefighter from breathing smoke.

We were already a little winded by the time we got to the top floor. As soon as we stepped into the hall, we were enveloped in heavy black smoke. It was bad enough to put the masks on. An initial search revealed nothing but more smoke and nearly zero visibility. Things were much worse than they appeared from outside, certainly. I got worried when I saw that it was impossible to see my partners' flashlight beams if they were over three or four feet away. I got everybody back together and told them to go back outside. I didn't want anybody getting separated from the group and getting lost in the smoke. We hadn't had time to bring in any safety lines or anything like that yet. It was still very early. No tactical decisions had been made. We went back down for fresh tanks and more men. I knew by then I wouldn't be getting back to those ribs any time soon.

I reported what we'd found up there: bad conditions,

heavy smoke, zero visibility, no flame found yet. The ladder was operating by then and more off-duty people had arrived. Most of the people on my shift were there, including my boss, who took charge of the ladder. My two duty partners were there, getting their turnouts on, getting ready to go up. I got another tank and climbed on the ladder platform and caught a ride to the roof. There was a wide ledge, maybe twelve feet or so, outside the fifth floor. The captain of the shift on duty got off on the ledge and the rest of us went on to the roof. My boss let us off and went back down for more men and equipment. His steady, up-and-down trips, five stories high, ferrying people and supplies, would go on unceasingly for the next few hours.

The fire needed to be ventilated—that is, an opening of some sort made in the building to let the buildup of heat and smoke out, to improve visibility conditions so the fire could be located and attacked. It was a long time before that happened.

We started another search of the fifth floor. We appeared to be in a hall that was built in a large rectangle with numerous doors that opened into offices. What we didn't know was that the fire was in the very center of the building, in a lounge area that had only two doors. We wasted an enormous amount of time checking for fire in the outlying offices, working by feel and touch in a place that was solid black to the eye, a place growing uncomfortably hot. We had a bad fire, it was rapidly worsening, and we didn't have it located, although we were searching as diligently as we could. Bells started ringing on the tanks, and I realized that it might be possible for some of us to become disoriented in the smoke, run out of air, and have to pull the mask off, and maybe never make it back to safety and fresh air. We went back outside to count heads and then we climbed on up to the roof.

An entry saw with a gasoline engine had been sent up in case we decided to cut a hole in the roof, but the roof was constructed of gravel over tar paper over concrete. Something else had to be done, something quick. The smoke had to be let out of the building right away, before a bad fire got any worse, before the heat intensified any more. The only thing we saw was the windows.

More people had come up, along with hoses and nozzles and ropes and more airpacks. I went over to the ladder and told my boss about the conditions, that it was evidently a bad fire and getting worse, and that we were going to have to break some windows on the fifth floor. He listened and nodded, and went down for tools.

I don't know what all happened then. Adrenaline. The next major event was the arrival via the ladder of two men with a fire ax and a heavy pry bar. I got back on the ladder platform and went with them down to the fifth-floor ledge and we walked to the corner window, a huge pane of dark glass that looked very expensive. Hundreds of people were standing below on the ground. Red and blue lights were flashing everywhere down there. The ladder was running at a high throttle, and hoses had been laid from the pumpers to the building so that we could boost the water pressure inside the standpipe system. I took a deep breath and swung the heavy pry bar as hard as I could at the window. It bounced off.

I braced my feet, tightened my helmet strap, turned the point of the tool to the glass and tried my best to shatter it. It bounced off.

I'm no ball player, never have been. But I brought the heavy bar around from behind my back with both hands gripping it like a baseball bat and delivered all the weight of it to the center of the window and it caved in in large jagged pieces. We were immediately engulfed in a roar of dense black smoke that barreled out over us so heavily that we had to move out of it and go on to the next window. People on the ground were yelling.

We eventually broke nine windows in a row all down that side of the fifth floor, walking down the ledge, swinging the pry bar in, knocking the sharp edges of glass out of the casement. More men were delivered to the ledge and we established our entry and exit route: through a window halfway down the side, step down into a nicely upholstered Law School dean's desk chair, walk across his desk and papers, drop onto the floor, try to find the fire. I think we knocked a lot of things over. A forward command post was set up on the ledge, and the captain relayed his orders for men and equipment via walkie-talkie back to the assistant chief, who directed the ground operations from the parking lot.

That trip I went in without a mask, because the smoke was lifting a little, even though the temperature seemed to have increased. I knew that was because the fire was getting a fresh supply of oxygen, but that's something you have to deal with when you ventilate. If you can go on in and make your stop, it doesn't make a shit.

Our pumpers were feeding the standpipe system, and we got the little piss-ant hose off the rack and stretched out the line. We thought the fire was right in front of us, and we were going to crawl our way up to it and find it and fight it. But we couldn't get the valve turned on. We tried and tried and even hammered on it with spanner wrenches, but we couldn't get it to open. We sent somebody out for a pipe wrench and then got it turned on, but blew the hose completely out of the coupling from the tremendous pressure our pump operators were sending through the pipe.

It took a little while to shut it off, take off the burst hose, and put our own nozzles and hose on it. But when we had that done, we put on fresh tanks and went down the hall in a group, close to the floor. We knew where it was now, back there in that lounge.

The air was burning our ears, even down that low. All of us crawling and sliding in the water, going inside a door where the thing was feeding and getting bigger. That is a special place to be in, with men in a burning building, where you can only barely hear one another talking behind the masks, where the glow of the fire makes a light on the masks around you, where you are all panting and pulling on the hose and trying to be as small and concentrated as possible, trying to do the job. Sometimes you reach a stage of near exhaustion after only a few minutes.

All we could see was a hellish red light in front of us somewhere. But we could hear the damn thing. Everything around us was charred, the water we were crawling in was black and hot, and the only smell was that of heavy smoke. My partners had the nozzle and I had my hand on their shoulders and we were inching forward, spraying water. We slipped on the tiles until we got to the carpet and then we pushed close to the fire, to that awful heat, until it came through our turnouts and our gloves and into our knees where we knelt in the hot water. Another bell started ringing and I hollered for whoever it was to get out. Somebody left and somebody came in on the line to replace him. We kept pushing forward, yelling, urging each other on.

You have to meet the thing is what it is. You have to do something in your life that is honorable and not cowardly if you are able to live in peace with yourself, and for the firefighter it is fire. It has to be faced and defeated so that you prove to yourself that you meet the measure of the job. You cannot turn your back on it, as much as you would like to be in cooler air, as much as you would like to breathe it. You have to stay huddled with the men you are with.

We whipped that fire's ass. It fought back, leaping and dodging the water, but we kept the nozzle open and on fog and rotated it in a counterclockwise manner due to the rotation and curvature of the earth, and the water was dispersed into tiny droplets by the turbojet nozzle. The droplets were converted into steam by the heat of the fire and steam is what put the fire out.

We pulled back for a breather and more people came in to mop up small fires and start salvage and overhaul.

In the Law School dean's office I saw my partners with sootstreaked faces, exhausted beer-drinking buddies with their coats open, lying on shards of glass in the floor with cigarettes in their hands. There was an unbelievable amount of talking and confusion. I lit my own cigarette, went back across the man's nice desk and out on the ledge, and told them we'd knocked it down.

It isn't until later that the real exhaustion sets in. They sent up some cold Gatorade that was delivered while the overhaul went on, while more men, fresh men, came up, while they ferried empty air tanks back and forth to Station One for refilling at the compressor, while men worked at the station filling the tanks, while the pump operators watched the gauges and engine temperatures, while the people in charge oversaw everything from outside and talked on their walkie-talkies, while the dispatcher manned the radio, while my boss carried the platform of the ladder up and down, over and over.

I sat down on the floor and smoked a cigarette and drank some Gatorade. We all looked at each other and just shook our heads.

Later we were told that it looked like a black tornado had come out of the building when we broke the first window, and that a man from the university's physical plant department had started tearing at his hair when we started breaking the windows because they cost $1,500 apiece.

Well, yeah. But it got the smoke out. Their fireproof building didn't burn down. And we were all still alive when it was over.

Ahhhhhhhhhhhhhhhhhhhhhhhhhhhhhhhhhhhhh. Off duty. How sweet it is. I'm in the process of building a patio, twelve feet by twenty-four feet, hand-laid brick with a roof over it. I'm laying a herringbone pattern, just like the one in the sidewalk in front of William Faulkner's house. I've been in this process for about four weeks. I foolishly thought it would only take five or six weeks, and now I see that it's going to take about sixteen or eighteen. Dove season will be open before I'm done.

It would be hard to explain how happy I am when I'm off duty. I'm so happy when I'm off duty, I could just lie down in the carport and kick and scream. But I don't do it. I have this room out here, on the other side of the carport, and when I'm off duty I'm able to go into this other room, which is actually another world, and write. I'm able to shuck off the other part of me and do this thing I have to do in this room I built just for myself. Or, I can say poot on it and build a patio.

I have children. Billy Ray, fourteen. Shane, ten. LeAnne, seven. Delinah would have been twelve now. There was also a miscarriage way back. Mary Annie put the tiny fetus in a clean margarine bowl and took it to the hospital with her.

We've had no greater share of hard troubles than other people I know.

We finally have our own house. We built it a few years ago, because we couldn't live in the house with Mary Annie's mother anymore, because it all came down to my writing, which I couldn't do over there, across the driveway. When her daddy, Preston, or Topknot, as everybody called him, died many years ago, everybody said the right thing to do was move in with her mother and take care of her and *her* mother, Pat, and I listened to the people who said those things and even believed them, being young and naive and not knowing that a man and his wife needed to form their own life together, since that's usually the plan, and it took some years and some heartbreak to find out moving in with Mary Annie's mother was not the right thing to do.

I left one time, stayed four days with a friend I worked for on my off days setting out baby pine trees. I had been out one night, drinking, and Mary Annie had cooked a supper for me that I hadn't been there to eat. Later on, when I finally came in, and had fixed my plate and was about to carry it out to the living room, words were said. I had told her I'd be home in time for supper. She was hot over my going out drinking instead. I said something smart and she doubled up her little fist and caught me square in the jaw with a decent right hook. It didn't hurt that bad. I've been hit by marines and sailors much harder, but of course I dropped my plate on the floor, food everywhere, gravy, all that. I told her I'd be packing my shit immediately, which I did. There was one brief and insane struggle over a .22 rifle. I took all the bullets away from her. Shane was a fat little baby, black-headed and born mad at the world, crying every night all night long. Our lives were not easy then.

Four days were all I could stay away from them. I crawled back in the window one night and I've been with them ever since.

I've just been out in the gloam with my cousin. We've been riding around drinking a few beers, what my mama used to call "acting ugly." If you don't know what the gloam is, you can find out by reading some James Street. He's a Mississippi writer who's been dead for a long time, but he knew what it felt like when the sun went down and left about an hour of light before dark. It's the very best time to ride around and listen to some music. Run over snakes. We try to do it several times a week in the summer. A man's got to have a bro to run with sometimes.

If I go to a bar, Ireland's is the bar I go to. On a

really lively night you'll see drunk women falling down, fights and potential fights, sweet young things and big-butted women, cowboys and construction workers and firefighters. I probably spend more time at Ireland's than I should. I live out in the county, out here in the land of the Big Sky country. I live at the edge of a river bottom, and the clouds can go all mushroomy and marshmallowy late in the afternoon and loom up big and white in the sky so that they can capture your attention. We have our own catfish pond, and we feed our fish. Billy Ray does.

He got a little red wagon for his first Christmas. The first time I pulled him in it, I pulled it too fast—he couldn't even crawl yet—and flipped him backwards out of it on his head. I thought I'd killed him. I nearly killed Shane, too. I was bringing some firewood into the house one night and he was right between my legs holding onto me and jabbering and all. He was only about eighteen months old. The stick of wood weighed about fifteen pounds. And I dropped it right on top of his head. I don't know how it kept from killing him. You get these babies, these little miracles, and then you do something stupid that nearly kills them. You think, Jesus, kid, you need somebody better than me to take care of you.

There are a lot of cows out in the pasture. It's pleasurable to sit out there on the partly finished patio and watch them grazing around on the green grass and all. It's pretty motivating. When you get that peace and tranquillity locked into you, anything is possible. We fish in the river. We live a life in harmony with nature and are glad we're here. I think it's a pretty wonderful life, what I've undertaken here. Spend time with my firefighting buddies for twenty-four hours and then come home and spend more time with my family for forty-eight hours and then turn around and do it all over again. My life is in cycles. I don't know what it would be if it wasn't.

I've skipped a day of duty, which is pretty good when you can do it. I'd probably skip every day of duty if I could. I'd lie around here and write and work on my patio all the time if I could. I want to be through with it before fall if I can. It took two solid weeks just to shovel the dirt out of it. LeAnne came out one day and said why didn't I just dig it a little deeper and make a swimming pool out of it? Some day some little boy's going to look at her bottom in a pair of blue jeans and come over here to take her out and I'm going to get him down in the kitchen floor and just beat the shit out of him.

I've been cleaning out my writing room and I've got lots of problems with insects. We've got spiders around here like you wouldn't believe. I've murdered thousands of the unhatched little mothers in the last few days. It's like Spider Heaven over here. Also Mouse Heaven. I think it comes from building a house in a pasture. The first year it was Tick Heaven, until I got some Dursban and went to murdering millions. We had them crawling in the windows, clambering over the carpet, clinging all over the furniture. We were afraid we were going to have to burn the house down just to get rid of them. It made us feel like inferior people, although we knew it wasn't our fault. When company was over we'd be shifting our eyes around, looking to see if one was walking. We didn't want them sucking on our guests.

I had a fight with a mouse a while back. I was sitting in the living room late one night, listening to the stereo, and I saw a mouse run from the living room closet to the bathroom. I knew I had him hemmed up. There's only one way out of the bathroom. I got the broom and went in there and shut the door, and sure enough, there he was, trying to decide which way to run. He ran up under the vanity and I stabbed at him a couple of times with the broom, and then he quickly hid under a pile of towels in the corner. I beat the shit out of that pile of towels, and he ran out, started trying to climb the wall in the corner. And then the little bastard turned and *attacked* me! He was leaping in the air, squealing. I swung at him but I missed each time. I started getting a little panicky. I whomped the carpet behind him as he ran to the back part of the bathroom, him hopping and leaping, both of us excited, him for his life, me just to rid my house of vermin. I was determined to get him. He cunningly hid behind the commode and I eased over into the bathtub and started whipping the hell out of him, poking him, and he went crazy and darted out from there. I chased him back into the front part of the bathroom and he hid in the pile of towels again. I beat on it and beat on it and beat on it, and finally he ran out and tried to find a place to hide. I poked and stabbed and really got pretty excited. I started breathing hard and I know my blood pressure went up. He ran out of the corner and into another corner and tried to sneak past me in the wide open. I swung at him and he *attacked* me again! I had to retreat, and I climbed up on top of the vanity that time. I tried to whip the hell out of him from up there, but he ran back into the rear part of the bathroom again. I gave him a little time. Everything was quiet. Both of us waiting. I knew he knew he was fixing to get killed. I really hated it, but I just couldn't let him go. He'd breed others, and they'd run wild all over the house. I poked my nose around the corner. He was hiding behind the commode again, just his nose sticking out, looking and listening for me. I got in the bathtub again and started jabbing him. He ran out and got back into the front part of the bathroom again. He had little shiny black eyes. Everybody else in the house was asleep and didn't know what I was going through, trying to murder one mouse. He dove into that pile of towels again and I whipped the hell out of it again for a while, and when he finally ran, I dragged all that stuff out of the corner so he couldn't hide in there again. I was planning my strategy, see. Not giving the enemy any place to hide. Sweep and destroy. He went back to the corner again and I flogged futilely at him when he ran by and went back behind the commode. I was getting a little tired of him not giving up. I saw that he wasn't going to just let me kill him, that he was going to fight for his life. I stepped back into the bathtub. I felt pretty ridiculous. *Real* ridiculous. If I'd had a BB gun I'd have just shot him, like Daddy used to do them in the kitchen when I was a kid. I knew that he was leaping toward me just out of desperation, like when the bear turns on the dogs at the brushpile. I poked and jabbed some more and got him to run. He was trying to climb into the cabinets, but they're new and tight, and he couldn't get inside. Finally I whopped him one good hard one, and he kicked backwards and fell out in the floor jerking. I laid it on him then, just beat the crap out of him. He kept trying to get up and run. I couldn't see how something so little could have so much heart, and I felt sort of cowardly. He put up a pretty good fight for a mouse. I was breathing really hard by then. I couldn't believe it. I almost thought I was going to have a stroke. Over one little mouse. When he stopped moving, I stopped hitting him.

I scooped him up in a dustpan and carried him outside so the dogs or the cats could eat him. I checked his balls. They were pretty big. No telling how many mice he'd have fathered in my house. I'd seen baby ones before, little pink naked mewling ones my mother-in-law found living in her cedar chest one time. I threw them over the fence. I guess mice have a hard time of it.

I threw this one out on the carport and looked at him, dead, wanting to live. I could hardly get over it. It made me uneasy for a long time.

It was a lovely summer afternoon, about three or four in the afternoon, and the line of stopped cars we had been passing for the last two miles made a steady rushing sound in the windows of the fire truck, and the wreck was below us, finally in sight, about a mile away, at the bottom of a very steep hill we were going down, and we were doing sixty-five, and we had no brakes.

Uncle Bunky and I had already braced ourselves to be killed. I felt fairly sure that we were going to die, and the only thing I was wondering was how many of the people who had driven the Highway Patrol cars and the ambulances at the bottom of the hill where the wreck was were going to die, too, when we slammed into them, at sixty-five. The truck I was driving weighed many tons, and it carried 750 gallons of water that weighed eight pounds per gallon, and I knew that the brake shoes had "faded away" from the drums from the repeated use of them, and I was bearing down on the brake pedal with everything I had and the truck wasn't slowing down any. Down below us, there was a whole crowd of flashing blue and red lights and stopped traffic stretching away on the other side as far as the eye could see. A truck was overturned in the middle of the road, and I told Unkie that we weren't going to make it. Looking back, I guess I should have been talking to Jesus instead of him.

Like I said earlier, it was a fine summer afternoon, but I never believed all that Indian shit about it being a good day to die. I did not want to slam into that group of emergency vehicles. I pumped the pedal and it didn't give anything back. I downshifted and the sound of the stopped cars kept rushing in the windows. We had already driven nearly twenty miles to this wreck, passing cars, hogging the road, running people off the road, and I had come upon it a little too fast, not knowing exactly where it was, just on Highway 30. I told Unkie that I thought the only chance we had was to pull the MicoBrake just before we got there, which would lock all the tires down if there was anything left. I kept downshifting, trying to slow down, pumping the brake. It still didn't feel like I had anything, and suddenly I was given a miracle, because the pedal had something under it, and we slowed down some and I downshifted some more and we swung in nonchalantly beside the wreck and parked without telling any of the assembled rescue people how close they had come to another disaster.

You never know what to expect. You just get out and deal with whatever they have called you to. You are the professional, that is your job. You hold the answers in your hands and your mind. There is always a victim to be extricated on a call like this, sometimes a crushed and dying person whose life may depend on what you do and how you do it. What we were looking at that day was a dump truck that had been carrying a load of lime. It had swerved to miss an oncoming car, and the truck had flipped. There were several tons of lime on the road. The trailer was on its side, but the frame had twisted and the cab was upside down with the roof resting on the highway centerline. The driver had come out with the windshield. His wife, or his woman, or whatever she was to him, was inside the cab, underneath all that iron and steel.

Most wreck victims are in shock when you get there. They're walking around in a daze, or lying on the side of the road with a blanket over them if somebody is there who knows how to treat for shock and thinks to do it. This man, a middle-aged black man, was in shock, and up and walking around. I could see the woman through the large hole where the windshield had been. She had on a red shirt and a pair of blue jeans. There were a whole lot of people standing around watching. There always is. I dropped down on my belly in the broken glass and diesel fuel and crawled under the truck with her. I dreaded seeing what I would find.

She was a young woman, probably less than thirty. She was flat on her back on the roof, and her main problem was that she was caught by the dash in the one place a lady surely ought not to be caught, and pinned effectively with her legs on either side of the sharp ridge of the dash. She had a broken nose, and aside from that, and aside from being terrified, she seemed to be all right.

I talked to her and told her that we were going to get her out. I held her hand. She gripped my hand with a strength born out of fear. I told her that I had to feel of her, that I had to check for broken bones, for her to please not think anything about it, that I was a firefighter, that I was trained in my job and that I had to check for what injuries she might have. She squeezed my hand and told me that she understood. She said, Don't leave me. I said, I won't.

How would I have been if I had been in her place? A truck upside down on top of me after that awful thing happened? She was pretty cool. I checked her legs and arms. Nothing seemed to be broken. I asked her if she had any internal pain. She said nothing was hurting her but her nose. And this other, she said. I kept holding her hand. I told her that help was on the way, but that was a lie. Sometimes you have to lie to them to make them stop believing that they're going to die. I knew we hadn't brought a damn thing with us that could lift that truck off her. So we just lay under there at first and talked. She told me what had happened, how the wreck had happened, how it had happened so fast. It was very hot, and we were both sweating. I could see the faces of nurses and ambulance attendants peering in the broken windows at us.

What we needed was a crane, but we didn't have one on Engine 8. I told her that I had to leave for a few minutes, but that I'd be right back. I crawled out from under the truck and stood up. Traffic was completely blocked for miles each way. I called Unkie over to the side and told him that her ladyhood was caught tight and that we were going to have to jack up the truck or something. I asked him what he wanted to do. He was the shift chief, I was just a lieutenant. We had a small hydraulic extrication device called a Ram Tool and he said he guessed we'd better get it out of the truck.

I got it out and set it up under the wreck and all it did was blow a gasket. There was more weight than the little hydraulic piston could move. The woman kept looking at me with those eyes while I lay next to her and jacked the handle of the Ram Tool until it blew the gasket. I lit a cigarette and she asked me for one. She wanted to know first if it was dangerous to smoke under there. I told her that diesel fuel had a low flash point. I stayed under there and we smoked a cigarette apiece.

I said, Listen. I'm going to try and move you. I told her I didn't think her hip was broken. She said she didn't think her hip was broken, either. I told her that I was going to try and slide her out from under that dash. I told her that if it started hurting her, for her to tell me. She said she would.

I tried and tried. I hooked my hands in her belt loops and pulled and pulled, but there was no moving her. She was stuck tight, and embarrassed, and she giggled a little, maybe from shock, maybe from this white boy lying under a smashed truck with her trying to get her vagina unhung. Mutually we decided that we weren't doing her any good. When I crawled back out that time, I figured traffic was backed up all the way to the Union County line.

Miracles happen sometimes. We'd already had one, so I never expected two. A convoy of National Guard trucks was backed up somewhere in the line, and one of them had a crane. The Highway Patrol brought them up and into position and they parked next to the wreck. I crawled back under there with her and told her what was about to happen, that they were going to wrap a steel cable around the cab of the truck and tighten it up slowly and that I was going to hold onto her and slide her out the second the pressure lifted. I think she dreaded that. I think maybe she thought they might lift it a few inches and then drop it back down on her and crush her. I didn't tell her that I was afraid that might happen, too. The cable came in, and I passed it around the body of the truck, and sent the hook back out, and they tightened it. We didn't say anything. The cable creaked. The truck shifted. She squeezed my hand. There was the groaning of metal. The dash slowly lifted and I grabbed her belt loops in my hands and slid her backwards, and suddenly many hands reached in and caught her with me and we pulled her out onto the highway and she was free.

We stood around for a while. They attended to her and she was able to stand. She was crying, but from happiness, glad to be alive, and she came over to me, this young woman who had lived and not died, and she put her arms around me, and she hugged me. I think maybe now that there was even a gentle kiss on my cheek. I know that she stood off from me for a second, just before she climbed into the ambulance, with her arms on my shoulders, and looked at me. Then they took her away.

Unkie came over and said, You did good, Brown.

My dog, Sam, sometimes makes mistakes. He once dove off a sixty-foot bridge into a river because he thought there was some ground on the other side of the railing. He looked very foolish from where I was standing, down on the river bank, sixty feet below, his eyes moving left and right in bewilderment as he fell, his legs dogpaddling the sky. It was a mere stroke of luck that he wasn't killed instantly by landing on the bank. The river was low and only about ten feet wide that day, but he hit right in the middle of it, swam over to me, puked a couple of times, and then he was all right.

He's short, sleek black, half Welsh corgi and half black-and-tan feist. He's supposed to be a squirrel dog. He's a sexual virgin and has a look of intelligence with his upright pointed ears that lies. He's terrified of thunder and lightning, will crawl up in your lap and cry over it, but will fight and kill snakes and rats. He's an excellent mole dog.

I had another dog a while back that came into heat, and even though I wanted Sam to get her pregnant and make some more like him, he couldn't do it. He thought it was on the outside of her left rear leg, and he hunched on that until he almost dislocated her leg. He ran her completely off. I can't find her, and I haven't seen any buzzards circling.

We have a lot of fun with him and one of the things we do to him is pick up Pooch, our other dog, a white beagle, and hug him and push Sam back, and before long he'll perform these incredible leaps four feet off the ground, snapping at Pooch's balls, and crying all the time. It's really enlightening to watch it and wonder about the emotions of dogs. It's pure jealousy, and you wouldn't think a dog would know jealousy. It opens up other ramifications, like, do they know heartbreak? And loneliness? And angst? I think they do. I think they know fear and greed and love, impatience and uncertainty.

These are just some of my random thoughts on dogs.

I retired back in January. And this is September. The Season of the Dove has already been upon us for several weeks now. You can get your driver's license in Mississippi when you turn fifteen, so Billy Ray can go hunting whenever he wants to in my little brown truck. Shane is eleven and wanted me to take him out to shoot at some doves. He didn't have any shells, so I went to town and got him some at the pawn shop one day, but ended up paying $150 for a used Fender electric guitar before I could get out of there. That afternoon we went over to a soybean field right across the creek from our house, almost our back yard, and sat down in a row with the green plants right in front of our faces, but only four doves flew over and we missed every one. I don't hunt like I used to.

Things have changed some. Pooch, our little white beagle, got killed. Somebody ran over him down on the highway. So now I make Billy Ray lock Sam in the utility room with the deep freeze and all my tools whenever he takes off on the four-wheeler for the river bottom. We don't want anything happening to Sam. We've still got high hopes of getting some puppies out of him if we can ever figure out a way. His legs are short, for one thing, and that gives him some trouble *mounting up,* so to speak, but I think personally that it's unnatural for a male dog not to know where a female dog's thing is. And I don't know if a vet can artificially inseminate a dog or not. I know they can do it with horses and cows, but I don't know how they'd extract the semen, unless you could get him to have a wet dream. I do know for a fact that Sam had a wet dream on top of Billy Ray's bed the other day, around the middle of the afternoon. Mary Annie—I didn't see it personally—said he was asleep, and jerked and whined for a long time, and then ejaculated. She thought it was about the cutest thing she'd ever seen. I wished he'd had it stuck in something that would have done all of us some good.

I took him to Ireland's when he was about six inches long. I didn't tell anybody I was taking him to town and Mary Annie (MA from here on out) looked all over the place for him. I had him buttoned up inside my shirt with just his little black head sticking out, and I'd go sneaking up behind girls, with a beer in my hand, rubbing his cold little nose on their bare arms to give them sort of a goose. He's been like one of my kids ever since.

I suppose I could go back and rehash some old fires, exciting things that happened. That happened, and a lot of boring things happened. A firefighter has to face boredom as well as danger. There are all sorts of other things that happen, stuff you wouldn't think about, like club ladies in town who suddenly decide that the fire stations ought to have flowers and shrubs planted all over everywhere, who then call up either Uncle Chiefy or the mayor, and the end result is that the firefighters have to get out and plant flowers and shrubs when they could be inside catching some S and V on HBO or Cinemax. Another bad thing about the fire service is that you have to see dead people, burnt-up people, and people who have died of smoke inhalation and people in car crashes who are already dead or who are dying in cars you're trying to take apart with the Hurst Tool while about fifty other people stand around and watch you and offer advice. I never dealt with it very well. I was never able to close my eyes and go to sleep after something like that, not any time soon after.

One of the reasons I liked being a firefighter was that I always had the feeling that I was helping people. I don't mean like helping get a cat out of a tree or anything. I mean like stopping somebody's house fire, where they were going to lose all their possessions, all their pictures, things that couldn't be replaced. A fire in a house is an awful thing to see. What the heat does to the things in that house is incredible. You can have a fire in the back of a house and it will melt a telephone in the front. Fire does strange things. A fire can kill you without ever touching you. It can raise the temperature of the air inside a building to a superheated level that will be fatal on the intake of the first breath. Most people who die in fires don't burn to death; they die from smoke inhalation that kills the respiratory system. That's why the fire service is always going on and on about smoke detectors. These little ten-dollar gadgets are one of the truly wonderful inventions of man. They'll wake you up from a deep slumber so that you and your family and your dog or cat or whatever can get out of the house in time to live and call the fire department. If this sounds like a public service announcement, it is. If you don't have one, buy one today. They make great Christmas gifts. Plus they're cheap. Give a gift of love to a loved one you love. End of announcement.

The worst thing I ever saw was either two babies and their grandmother burnt to death, to nothing, to just charred black lumps that had to be picked up out of smoking rubble, or a guy who wasn't dead yet who was mashed half in two by a truck. I saw a lot of death, and I worked at a small department in a little Mississippi town. It may sound cold, but the dead who were already gone never bothered me as much as the living ones, who were in great amounts of pain and shock, who had to be assured that yes in fact they were not going to die but were going to live if they would just take it easy and relax. You cannot think about a person's pain and do your most efficient job; if your feelings about his feelings are weighing on your mind more than how best to remove his crumpled car door from around his body, you're not doing him any good and should probably step aside and let somebody else operate the tool.

Remove the car from the victim, not the other way around. You can be faced with anything. A car upside down on top of two people, one dead, one alive. A head-on collision, two dead, two alive, one each in each car. A car flipped up on its side against a tree, the driver between the roof and the tree. A burning car with live occupants trapped inside.

Rolling on a call has been likened to soldiers going into combat. I never had a feeling any better than I had when driving my big pumper through the streets of Oxford at three or four in the morning, while everybody was sleeping, while the streets were deserted except for an occasional police cruiser, with the lights flashing just yellow caution at the intersections, wheeling that big red truck like all little boys would like to and some will grow up to, like me, and knowing that they were all asleep while we were up, taking care of the city of my birth, watching over them, there and ready to protect them and help them if they needed us. I know that sounds sappy as hell. I don't give a shit if it does.

It's a summer night in the late 1980s and we're up on a bridge outside of town. The two men ahead of us in the decapitated car have been nearly decapitated themselves, and I'm reluctant to walk up there and see them in their death and blood. Some of the younger boys I work with don't feel like this, but I've seen enough of it already. I take the cops' word for it and go back to the van and get on the radio and cancel the rescue unit that's screaming toward us.

Later I'll take this incident and put it into a novella and act like I made it up, but here they both are, one of them gasping for breath, and he'll die soon, en route to the hospital in the ambulance, and the driver is already dead. He hit a tractor-trailer that was crossing the road—he was doing about ninety—and slid all the way under it and out the other side for 105 feet. The cops have the tape out and are measuring the single skid mark, which means only one brake shoe was working. We've got our pumpers parked in the middle of the road with all our lights flashing, and we were probably eating something or watching something just before we were called out to witness this.

The ambulance arrives. There's nothing for us to do but wait around to wash the broken glass and debris off the road after a wrecker tows the car. The EMTs will transport the dead and the dying. The cops need some chalk and they don't have any, so I get back in the van and ride up to the main station for it. I keep thinking about the guy with his head cut off. The business I'm in, you can never tell where it will lead you. One day somebody wants you to get a cat out of a tree and the next day some kid may be burning up inside a house. The night we went into C. B. Webb, a housing project in town, when three apartments were on fire, with flames coming through the roof, the people standing out in the yard told us on our arrival that there were some kids trapped inside. We fought our way through fearsome rooms of fire, knocking the flames down everywhere, climbing a black staircase to the top floor, where there were only burned mattresses and charred walls and no bodies to be found. We found out later that one guy had jumped from the top floor, had hit a clothesline on the way down, had luckily broken only one leg, and had somehow managed to run off. He had been standing in a window broken from heat, and the people on the ground told him to jump or die.

As it turned out, they gave him good advice. He wouldn't have survived what had gone on up there.

I never laid my life on the line. That day when those two little kids and their grandmother burned up, I was out at the elementary school giving a fire extinguisher class with the chief, and somebody else had to drive my pumper to the fire. We got the call during the class, and I rode with Uncle Chiefy out there and we saw immediately that the house was falling in with fire. I was breaking in a rookie, and nobody had even told him to put his gloves on. He stood there in the yard and did all he could and blistered his hands badly while using an inch and a half hose. Then the house fell in and we were told that there were people inside.

It was late in the evening by then, winter. The ruins were smoking. Cops tried to keep screaming family members back. The smoke shifted in the rubble, and we all stood back, dreading what had to be done. The back door had been nailed shut for some reason. We couldn't have saved that house unless we'd gotten there early, long before it got so bad. Maybe they didn't have a phone to call us. Maybe they were taking a nap. Sometimes you can never save them. We wetted it down while crying and wailing women fought to be free from the police who held them. We entered the back side of the house and no words were said. The police had set out the body bags for us. It seemed like a hundred people were in the street, shouting and taking on in the most awful way. The smoke moved among the charred timbers and piles of ashes and glowing embers, and we had to find the things we were looking for. It was hard to tell, everything being so burned, everything looking so much alike. Only a firefighter or a victim of fire can tell you what a terrible thing fire can be.

There was silence among us as our people lifted the bodies out. The children were so small. I thought of my own. No words were said. Maybe it was February or March. The women were still screaming in the street. I wondered what my life would ever come to. These people had suffered a terrible death. I blamed it on poverty, and ignorance, and my not being at my station when the call came in, although the class the chief and I were giving could prevent things like this.

The lights of all the emergency vehicles blinked out in the street and even the cops wanted to turn their faces away from this. I know they have a hard time. People mess with them and they have to mess with the drunks. And once in a while they have to look at something with us.

A few days later, the man who was the father of the dead children came into the station to try and get his hands on a copy of the fire report so he could turn it over to his insurance company. A poker game was going on at our big table in the middle of the kitchen. This man had his cap in his hands, and his clothes were ragged. The betting went on, our boys never looking crossways at him, not knowing who he was. Their voices got louder while the man stood there patiently, waiting for the chief to find the report in the file cabinet. The man looked humbled by what had happened to him. His children had probably been buried quickly. The poker game went on and on and the man kept standing there with his cap in his hands, until finally, mercifully, Uncle Chiefy found the report and took the man back to the Xerox machine to make a copy of it. I never asked them to stop the game. Sometimes there was a weird callousness about the work we did. We couldn't let it get too close to us because we didn't want to be touched by it. We didn't talk much about the bad ones. When they happened, we dealt with them. Then we went back and ate or watched a movie or went on another call, or washed the trucks and polished the chrome. We got through our shifts and then we went home and went fishing or hunting or made love to our wives or played with our children. We hoped the bad things we saw would never claim us. We hoped we wouldn't die in smoke and flames or torn steel like the people we couldn't save.

I don't much think Sam's going to be able to get any puppies. I've just got my doubts about the little fellow. He nearly ripped MA's gown off her the other night. She got to pushing and shoving on Billy Ray where he was lying in the floor, playing with him, and Billy Ray got to hollering that she was hurting him, and Sam started growling and nearly went crazy protecting him and tore two holes in her gown and pulled one sleeve completely off her arm. I got to laughing so hard I couldn't even get up from the floor.

We mess with his head all the time just to see what he'll do. Just like with him and Pooch's balls. I think that may be connected, a dog that doesn't know how to make puppies trying to bite another dog's balls. I've never seen another dog do that. But I never saw a dog that didn't know how to make puppies, either.

I don't really understand it. He's got the hunching part down pat, witness his demented attack on the little gyp we had. He just didn't know where to stick it. You wouldn't think a four-year-old dog could be a virgin. You'd think he'd have found him a little, somewhere down the road. I guess it's our fault for making him live such a protected life. He never got to run with a pack. We're his pack. It looks like I'm going to have to set aside some time to think about it and try to arrange some way for him to get him a little. I feel like I'm depriving him. I'm sure some cute little girl dog would love to have him. Maybe a beagle with pretty eyes. Some laid-back bitch. We could fix them a little candlelit dinner in the carport, buy some of that good Alpo, arrange a nice blanket in the corner by the lawnmower.

Hell, I doubt if he'd let us watch.

The year is 1975. I have been a firefighter for less than two years, and I'm in a 1974 red-and-white LTD, speeding down through the Mississippi Delta to light a Christmas Tree this summer night. There are about six other off-duty firefighters in the car with me, and it's ten o'clock in the morning, and we're all drinking beer. Actually some of us are getting a little happy. We've stopped at a beer store in Batesville and we're having a wonderful time, heading off into adventure.

We come down out of the hills and flatten out into the Delta where there are few trees and thousands of acres of cotton growing. The heat lies in ripples over the land but we have the air conditioner going full blast. I feel myself getting a little woozy and I know it's going to be a long day.

The bad thing about drinking beer on a trip to a fire

school is that eventually you're going to have to start making pit stops. It's best to hold it for as long as you can, because once you start peeing, that's it. Before long you'll be stopping all the time.

The first one we make is behind a cotton pen on a long deserted stretch of road with few houses. The Highway Patrol would frown on our actions if they happened to come by, so we all try to hide behind the little building. It's still a long way to Greenwood, but there are plenty of beer stores between here and there. Just how many, we don't know yet, but we'll find out. We hope to arrive in Greenwood around one, maybe two. We were supposed to arrive in Greenwood around twelve. But we don't have a whole lot of responsibility about us on a trip like this. The trunk is packed full of our turnout gear, our coats and boots and helmets and gloves. I've never been to a Christmas Tree before, and I'm a little nervous about it. We've been told that the temperature will reach 1,500 degrees.

We stop at a couple more beer stores. We go past the penitentiary, Parchman, see the high walls and the barbed-wire fences, and we shake our heads, glad we're not in there.

We notice that the price of beer goes up the deeper we get into the Delta. It's nearly twice what we pay for it in Oxford, but we don't complain. We can't stop now. But we're having to stop the car every twenty minutes because some of us have stronger bladders than others, and when the pain gets too bad, it doesn't matter where we are. We'll leap out behind trees, jump down in ditches, while the others sit in the car with the windows down and hoot and scream and throw beer cans. We're an accident looking for a place to happen.

We roll into Greenwood an hour late, all of us happy, and find the classroom and walk in as all heads turn to view the latecomers. They all shake their heads. They all know we're those crazy fuckers from Oxford. The class has been underway for some time. The man is explaining the properties of Liquid Propane gas, LP, and it's no laughing matter. Three Vicksburg firefighters have recently been killed in an LP explosion, burned to death and beyond recognition, a fire truck destroyed. We look at slides of what was left of their turnouts. We're told that we don't want to see the slides of the men who had worn them. We sit all the way to the back of the room, and we don't take notes because none of us thought to bring notebook or pencil. The class goes on and on and we're hungry and still thirsty.

We're told to be back just before dark, and then they turn us loose on Greenwood. We decide to go looking for something to eat.

The place to eat turns out to be a bar that serves hamburgers and things. We all go in and order beer and food and stay there most of the afternoon. We figure it doesn't make any sense to sober up now, so we don't.

When dark arrives, we're in a parking lot with a new lime-green fire truck, maybe a Seagrave or a Mack, and about a hundred other firefighters from cities all across

Mississippi. The State Fire Academy is teaching this course. A large LP gas truck is parked off to one side, and in the center of the parking lot there is a big framework of metal pipes that resembles the rough shape of a Christmas tree, with a base about fifteen or twenty feet in width. A line has been laid from the gas truck to the tree, and the Greenwood Fire Department's pumper has charged the hand lines. A flaming rag will be laid on an arm of the tree, and the gas in the truck will be turned on, and a ball of fire about twenty feet tall will erupt and intensify, and we will go up to the thing with only our hoses and turnouts for protection, and we will shut it down while holding the fire at bay.

One group of firefighters gets up to be first in line on the hoses, but we step up and tell them that we want to go first. We man the hoses and the Oxford firefighters pick the man who will have to crawl up and shut off the valve, who happens to be me.

The whole town has turned out to see this. The pumper is throttled up, adrenaline kicks in with a rush, the hoses are as hard as iron. Two groups of three men form on each side, and I hang back with the group on the left, my position the last one in the line. Some instructors from the academy stand with us. There is no joking or laughing now. One little fuckup and somebody will be burned badly. Everybody is ready. A firefighter in full turnout gear walks to the pipe framework, the Tree, and lays a rag on it that has been soaked in kerosene. He lights it with a cigarette lighter and runs out of the way. The rag lies there burning, one small point of light in the night, and the man at the gas truck opens the valve. Holes have been bored in all the pipes, and the gas rushes out in small blue flames, dancing in tiny blue spots only for a moment. He increases the volume and all the flames come together into one, and it starts to roar and change color. The blue-and-white fire comes out like water under pressure and it completely obscures the pipes. It towers over our heads and the awful heat touches us where we stand, fifty feet back from it. The two groups open the nozzles of the hoses in a fog pattern, and we start forward. The instructors tell us to keep our heads down, make sure our face shields are down. Our collars are pulled up and snapped tightly around our throats, and the gauntlets of our gloves are pulled up over the sleeves of our coats.

The two groups walk closely together, meshing the two fog streams so that there is an unbroken barrier of cool water between us and the fire. We get closer and the flames push forward over the fog streams. The instructors call, Steady, steady now. We go forward until we stand two feet from the living ball of fire. It is incredibly bright now, the flames reflected on the face shields of my companions. All of us are relying on each other. We have to trust each other not to run. The instructor makes us stand there, steady, until he sees that we are holding the fire at bay, and then he points to me. I drop to my knees and go forward, and I crawl between his spread boots. The parking lot is brighter now than day. There is a valve right in front of the instructor's boots, and I lie on the wet black bright asphalt and reach out with my gloved hand, the killing fire right above me, the terrible heat right over my neck. I turn the valve swiftly until it closes and the fire diminishes, drops, goes out. I get up, go back to my position at the end of the hose, and we back away, wet, steaming, droplets of water obscuring our vision behind the face shields. We did it right. At other times, at other Christmas Trees in the future, in other cities, it will not be done right, and once I will see my training officer badly burned because of the fear of a stranger, and take on a scar on his forearm the size of an elbow patch, something he will wear forever, but this time, this first time, we do it right.

Our gig done, we head for another bar.

We're still in Greenwood and we're still in a bar and there is a band from California playing. They have lots of horns and a pretty female lead singer and we're dancing in our uniforms with all the women in the bar. Some of the other firefighters have joined us until there are so many firefighters that we have taken over the bar with our happy debauchery and our loud jokes.

There is a woman in this bar with a set of breasts that are spectacular, that are not to be believed, that have attracted the eyes of every man in the bar. She dances so fine that I think she has to be a professional dancer. I go over and dance with her, but I'm no match for her. I don't know what I'm doing, I'm just flopping and jerking my body around on the dance floor, making a fool of myself. Her breasts are as big as my head, but she's not a big woman.

She must be a go-go dancer. Before long she starts slinging me around like a rag doll. She seems stronger than me and I'm embarrassed. She finally slings me into a chair and oh how the boys do howl. I'm having a sinking spell. I don't feel very good and we're still a long way from home.

It's later still and we're drunker still, riding back up through the Delta, and the lights are on outside the prison camps, and they look smoky, and scary, and our driver gets on the car's PA system, which is hooked into the fire department radio, and announces through the outside speakers that WE WILL NOT PISS AT THIS TIME, 10-4, over and over, very loudly, loud enough to nearly wake the dead, in fact, and I hope nobody comes after us, that they won't lock us into the penitentiary for disturbing the peace.

We ride back up into North Mississippi and we're not so chipper now, some of us having sinking spells, some of us asleep. When we finally get back to Oxford, the fire station is dark and quiet, the men on duty asleep. I get in my car and go home, not to my home in my house trailer but to Preston's, my father-in-law's home, where MA is sleeping because I've been gone and she is pregnant with Billy Ray. I crawl into bed with her and she sleepily asks me how it was. I say it was okay, thinking about how I tried to dance with a go-goer, and I hold onto the round ball of her stomach, where Billy Ray sleeps and grows, and I wonder what he is, what he will be.

I've been sitting out in the woods trying to shoot a deer. I haven't shot one in about ten years. I'm a real lousy hunter. Like if I'm still-hunting, where you're supposed to be sitting there as still as the tree you're sitting against, not moving a muscle, planted there like a statue chipped out of marble, I'll be opening my Thermos and pouring more coffee, smoking cigarettes, thumping ashes all over myself. The deer are probably relieved when they smell me and know it's me.

Billy Ray was going to shoot one the other day. It ran up and stuck its head out from behind a tree, and he shot the damn tree. That's from not having much of a coach.

I used to be slapdab teetotally crazy about it. I lived in a tent for three weeks one time. Couldn't get enough of the woods. But I'm not like that now. Something came over me. Maybe I got too much of it when I was a kid. I still like to walk in a forest, but I'm not so crazy about killing anymore. The killing never was the thing for me, anyway. It was mainly just being out in all that beauty. There are few things prettier to me than an old hardwood forest. We just don't have them around here much anymore. They've all been cut down. Faulkner was right. He said the land would accomplish its own revenge on the people. I just wish it hadn't happened in my time. I saw what those woods were like. I walked in them, along their creeks, among the giant beeches riddled with squirrel dens. That's what this whole country used to be, what wasn't farmed. Big woods. Now the whole state's a pine tree. And the bugs are eating them.

It's bad to hate something like that and not be able to do anything about it except recycle your paper.

I really went hunting this morning just to take Shane. Today's Thanksgiving. Everybody's sacked out in there in the living room, ate too much turkey. I got the boys up early, way before daylight, and we went to Thacker Mountain. I don't mind Billy Ray going by himself. He's fifteen, has used guns plenty. Shane's only eleven and hasn't had very much experience, but he wanted to go bad, and since that's my job I took him to a good deer stand built in a tree and put him up in it and then climbed up and handed him the gun, and went off and left him. I rode the four-wheeler to another spot about ten minutes away and sat on the ground, drinking coffee, smoking, not really seriously hunting.

Rain dropped out of the sky all of a sudden about nine o'clock. I got up right away and got on the Honda to go after Shane, but I was soaked before I got there. I was thinking I'd have to walk back out in the woods to the stand and get him, but he'd already unloaded his gun and come down and was walking up the trail to meet me, dripping wet, grinning with his braces. The other day, my two boys and one of my fire-department partners rode on the four-wheeler, all at the same time, and tore off the right rear fender, so now the wheel slung mud all over us and our guns. We went home. After I got the guns cleaned I made a pot of coffee and put on clean dry clothes down to my skin and got the paper and stretched out on the couch where it was warm, MA working in the kitchen, just contented as a wet beaver that we were all home together on Thanksgiving, football on, the nest complete. She's big on nesting.

At one time she thought I was a smartass, though. That's because way back before I even knew her, my cousin and I were riding to work in my mother's car, and went around this sharp curve in the rain, me driving too fast, not knowing how to drive too good yet, but eighteen, first real job, night shift at Chamber's, a stove factory, and the wheels skidded and I hollered, Hold on!, and wound up in his lap. We spun and ended up in the ditch on the other side of the road, pointed back the way we'd come, Mama's car slightly dented, two tires blown out. So I called a wrecker.

Before the wrecker got there, MA and her daddy and

mother came along in a black 1953 Chevrolet pickup in near-mint condition, and her daddy offered to pull me out, but I'd already called the wrecker and it was on its way. He offered several times and I said no thanks. I couldn't drive it anyway with those tires blown out.

She was about fourteen then. It was in 1969, one year before I joined the Marine Corps. When I saw her again she was eighteen and had great legs. That was the day I got discharged, in 1972. That day I was in the ditch, though, she thought I was a smartass. She claims I got smart with her daddy. I never did it. My mama didn't raise me to get smart with grownups. MA doesn't think I'm a smartass now, but for several years, apparently, she went around with the idea that I was a real asshole.

The day is hot and our turnouts are made of black canvas that draws the heat of the sun into us. We are all encased in black, our helmets black, our gloves, and the house before us is beginning to burn nicely. We stand in the overgrown yard with our hoses primed and ready, cigarettes in our fingers and the pumper throbbing at the curb. Our face shields are up. We're waiting for the fire to reach a stage of near-total involvement, where it's so bad we'll really be doing something when we go in and put it out.

Old houses, a whole street full of them, and the city of Oxford has made plans to burn them all down and renovate this section of the city, build new houses. We are the instrument by which this plan will be implemented.

Rob stands beside me with a charged hose, smiling his little smile in the heat at me.

You ready? he says.

I reckon, I say.

We button our collars tight and throw the cigarettes down and go across the yard, dragging the hose with us. You can't be a pussy now. The whole back side of the house is on fire and smoke is pouring from every window and every crack in the boards. It's pumping like smoke under pressure. We're not wearing our tanks. This is only a training exercise. We'll lie on the floor or go forward on our knees.

We go across the rotten porch as the smoke blocks out the sunlight, and the first sharp edge of it burns in our noses. As we clap our face shields down and go inside the house, the fire is running across the ceiling. It's almost like water the way it flows, every board and nailhead in the room consumed and living in bright orange fire. We get on our knees and the heat comes down to welcome us into its inner reaches. The house begins to roar and we open the nozzle and spray the burning overhead, and the fire banks down and we push forward to another room. The smoke makes our eyes tear and people are shouting outside. This is the real thing, as real as training can get, and our rubber boots slide in the water as we whip the fire back. The kitchen is consumed in flame, great walls of it, but the Elkhart Brass nozzle has the power to control it. We go from room to room, knocking it down, dealing with it, until the whole house smolders sullenly and goes out. We back out, our face shields covered with droplets of water, men helping each other, glad of what we're doing and glad we can do it.

We pull back into the yard to let the fire build up again. Other teams will go in after us and they'll fight the fire again and again until we all have a turn at it and then we'll let it burn the house down to the ground, create its own wind, howl and pop and have its way with the wood. Later we'll find ancient bricks from the chimney that were made in Oxford and have OXFORD cast into them.

I'm sitting in the yard having a cigarette, watching the house catch up again.

Rob says, Brown.

I look around. He opens up a charged two-and-a-half-inch handline and knocks my helmet off my head. I'm engulfed in a wall of water. He actually rolls me across the yard with it. It's hitting my ass like somebody's big fist. He rolls me over and over with it. The whole company stands and laughs and hoots. All I can do is roll up in a ball and wait for them to get tired of it. That nozzle is flowing 250 gallons a minute. And every one of them would save my ass should my ass need saving.

Somebody, some asshole jogging down the street one night, jogs into the fire station and swipes a walkie-talkie valued at eight hundred dollars. Then, over the scanner a few days later, somebody hears him trying to talk on it, but we never catch him. He probably throws the eight-hundred-dollar Motorola away. He probably thinks it's a CB radio or something. Thieving dumbass joggers loose on the streets of Oxford and inside our fire station while we're asleep.

Somebody, some asshole, picks up a captain's helmet at a fire we're working one day and then comes riding by the station a few days later on a motorcycle, wearing it. Another dumb asshole. Wally gets in the van and chases him down, makes him hand over the helmet. The guy is not charged for his crime. The helmet's worth about two hundred dollars.

A white raccoon gets into our dumpster one night and we see him making off with some of our garbage. We don't say anything, just let him go.

Somebody, maybe some asshole, maybe a friend of mine, dresses a bunch of fish and throws all the heads and guts into the dumpster and it's in the summertime and it stinks enough to make you want to puke. One of the captains chalks a note on the blackboard: If you dress fish at the fire station, please have the decency to put the "stinking remains" in a garbage bag so the rest of us won't have to smell it.

I hire a bunch of guys from the fire department, and we all build a house for my family and me in early 1986. We start in March and have it framed up, the roof on and the windows and doors in, in a few weeks. One cold afternoon when we've been putting tarpaper down on the roof, we knock off and Tex and I decide to ride around and drink some beer and peppermint schnapps. We get into my little pickup and ride around for a while and get a little high and then come around a curve in the road where the air is filled with white hair, simultaneously meeting a stopped car. We halt. The car has two girls in it. In the road in front of us is a doe deer, not dead, still kicking. We tell the girls, who are pretty horrified, that we'll take care of it. They drive off and we get out. Tex and I both have on insulated coveralls. A roadkill of this dimension is not to be ignored. Tex unfolds his pocketknife, pulls the deer's head over his knee, starts stabbing the hell out of the deer's throat and the deer dies. We've got fresh meat. We stand in the road in front of my headlights. A large brown stain starts growing on Tex's leg. It gets bigger and bigger. Cut yourself, Tex? I say. Nah, he says. It gets bigger and bigger. Believe you did, Tex, I say. Tex shucks down nearly naked in front of my headlights, and sure enough, he's stabbed himself in the leg. It's a pretty deep puncture wound. We just laugh in each other's faces and throw the deer into the back end of my pickup and haul ass uptown to the fire station.

We hang the deer on a ladder between two fire trucks. The guys on duty come out to the truck bay to laugh at us. The game wardens often come into the fire station for coffee and the newspapers and fried catfish, and it's risky business what we're doing. We skin the deer and quarter it and put it in the freezer, then go to Ireland's. I park my pickup right in front of the building, right next to the front door. I have a brand-new forty-eight-quart Igloo cooler with three six-packs of Budweiser in it. The cooler is worth about forty dollars, the beer about twelve dollars.

While Tex and I are inside wearing our bloody coveralls, drinking beer and trying to dance, somebody, some asshole, steals it.

. . .

We get several good meals out of the deer meat. We cook steaks one night, a roast another night, tenderloin with biscuits and gravy one morning. Then the ice machine messes up and somebody unplugs the wrong plug-in, and the deer meat thaws out and sits in the freezer for about two weeks, and when a couple of guys open the lid, they almost puke in the truck bay, and all our good deer meat is not something you'd even want to think about smelling.

Tex's leg heals nicely.

Hillbilly and I go out in his boat and run his trotlines. We have to go in folks' yards and promise them catfish in order to procure their catalpa worms. We go up to some old lady's house pretty often. She's real nice. We're the only ones she'll let get her catalpa worms. I climb the tree and knock the worms down by shaking the limbs hard, and Hillbilly grins because of all the abundance of catalpa worms here. It's coveted fishbait; unless you own your own trees you have to depend on the kindness of others, especially when you're running three hundred hooks. This sounds simplistic, I know, but we need three hundred worms for one baiting, and we're probably going to run the lines three or four times in the next few days. We need twelve hundred worms. This is serious fishing.

Hillbilly gets me out on the lake and has to test my woodcraft. I have to identify every little post and stump where we've got the lines tied. I have to lower or raise them to hide them from other people or let us be sure where they are, and I have to take off all the fish and bait up every hook while he sits in the back and runs the motor and drinks the beer I have furnished him, and he even wants to run the lines when the lake is choppy with wind and lightning and the water is coming in over the front in waves, so that I'm scared of dying a watery death although he does make me wear a life jacket.

Late one afternoon we have a fish on our line that we can't raise. We can feel him pulling, but we can't raise him. Hillbilly says Shit and I say *Shit!* We spend some time with him, pulling the line between our fingers, raising him up slowly, feeling him fight, and gradually we bring him to the surface and a carp that must be five feet long breaks water. He tears the hook out of his mouth and we sit back stunned.

We are at peace and at one with the wind and the water and the lake. We dress our catfish in the lake with filet knives and pack the filets into the shaved ice in the cooler. We're pretty damn happy. The sun is going down. All the hooks are baited. The lake is slick as glass and the beer is cold. We're not even thinking about a fire right now. Right now, we're not even firefighters. Right now we're fishermen and have the world by the ass. All these catfish are swimming under our hooks, and we'll be able to come back in the morning and take some more of them off and bait the lines up again. I'll have a case of trotline back before it's over. Hillbilly won't do anything but run the motor and tell me what to do. I have to do this because he knows where all the good spots are. He's only spent about forty years fishing on this lake. Plus he can kill big bucks every year. He's the greatest hunter and fisherman I've ever met. It's why I put up with him making me show him my woodcraft. Plus, he's got the boat.

We go to a house in Oxford down on North Seventh Street, the same neighborhood where we burned down all the old decrepit houses years ago to clear the way for improvement and progress. FHA has built low-cost housing, small brick homes, tiny yards, an improvement over the past in some ways. This house is full of a number of drunk or doped-up folks, and there is a fire behind the stove, and it's Saturday night. There is a leak in the pipe that feeds the appliance, and we pull the stove away from the wall and shut off the valve. The fire goes out. Some of the paneling is scorched, but the fire hasn't spread. We look around. Holes are poked in many of the walls, sheetrock and paneling alike. There is ruined food on plates on the counters. Cabinet doors are torn off. I go outside with a spanner wrench to shut off the main valve to the house and a drunk guy approaches me, calling me a white something or other. I hold up the wrench and show it to him. He backs off and leaves me alone, goes off somewhere into the darkness of the yard. I shut off the valve and go back into the house. The lady of the house, knit slacks, a saggy sweater, a filthy knit toboggan on her head, is drunk and cussing, Who this muddafucka what muddafucka muddamuddafucka. The smoke alarm has been sounding the whole time and it won't quit. I go outside to the utility room where she says the breaker box is and push the door open maybe ten inches, and then it stops, jammed tight with ironing boards and boxes of empty bottles, trash, clothes, beer cans, lawn chairs, junk and more junk. I step back out into the carport and look down to see bloody footprints all over the concrete, the footprints of a child, all red and perfectly outlined with the grain of the toes like fingerprints. The smoke alarm is still going off. Some child somewhere in this house or neighborhood has cut a foot badly and is walking around with it bleeding. I go back into the house. The smoke alarm is a piercing, pulsating series of short shrieks that hurt the eardrums. A bunch of drunks are still in the living room arguing hotly. My partners look nervous. They think knives may be pulled, guns fired, rightly so. Cap'n Brown, let's get the fuck out of here, they say. The smoke alarm is still going off and it won't shut up. I walk back into the hall where it's mounted and yank the wires loose. The son of a bitch shuts up then. We go back through the living room and there are plenty of young punks who smirk in our direction. The storm door doesn't have any screen or any glass. We tell them to call the gas company Monday. I don't know how they'll cook until then. We go out across the yard and Engine 10 sits throbbing at the curb, the side mirrors on the cab vibrating in their rubber mounts. I swing up into the driver's seat, take the pump out of gear, let off the airbrake. My partners climb into the front seat and the jumpseats mounted behind the cab. We're glad to be getting the hell away from here, but I can't help but worry about the child with the bleeding foot.

I swing the pumper away from the curb and step down hard on the pedal and she downshifts and then shifts up and we gain speed. I take off my helmet and the wind feels good in my hair.

Later, when we get back to the station, we find out that somebody has left a piece of equipment at the house, but naturally nobody wants to go back and get it. I'm the captain, I have to go back and get it. I get into the van I drive sometimes and tell them I'll be back in a few minutes. If they have a call while I'm gone, somebody can drive the pumper and I can meet them there in the van.

The drunks are still in the yard and in the house, still arguing. I don't say anything to them, I just get out and go into the house and pick up the rechargeable light that was left behind and head back out with it. Even the police don't like to come down here on Saturday night, and they have guns.

. . .

A house burns on North Seventh Street one night when I'm off duty, taking a vacation day. Uncle Bunky and Poot Man go through the front door and a corpse is on the floor, his eyes red and his dead hand reaching for the doorknob and the life-giving air six feet away.

A man who lives in a nice house in a nice neighborhood in Oxford has the not-nice habit of getting drunk and then falling asleep in bed smoking a cigarette. In several instances several months apart, he catches the house on fire. Another shift goes over and puts the house out both times, and his insurance company rebuilds it both times.

And one night, a few months later, when Poot Man is on duty, they get a call to the same house. This time he's on fire in his bed. He dies, despite their efforts. One month later, Poot Man resigns, and nobody blames him. There are days when all of us are taken to our limits.

Cats. They'll crawl up into the bathtub every time when the house catches on fire. I don't know why they pick that place to die, there among the shower curtain and the shampoo. Small dogs will do it, too, and it's not happy work to walk back out into the yard and tell the houseowners their pets didn't make it. Little Clyde and Buddy dead in there in the bathtub. It's pretty traumatic for the people involved, I'm sure. I don't even want to think about something happening to Sam. Sam I'm sure would raise all kinds of hell barking, then dive through a window like Rin Tin Tin. I've never seen a more intelligent animal than Sam. I've about decided that dogs can think. Or I think Sam can, anyway.

He'll try to talk, too, but he can't talk. He'll just holler a bunch of crazy dog stuff that *sounds* like he's trying to talk. And another thing is that he's ruined, spoiled, completely rotten. It's all MA and the children's fault. If Billy Ray leaves here, Sam will go over to Mamaw's (Esther Lee, MA's mama) and get her to let him inside. Then when he hears Billy Ray come home, no matter what time of night it is, he'll go to Mamaw's door and scratch and paw and whine until she has to get out of bed and let him out. Then before long you'll hear him whining and pawing and crying at our back doors, which are French-style, with glass in them, and it's really disgusting to have to listen to it. I don't mean that it has to be cold for him to want in. He just wants in. And MA and the kids will let him in. I don't let him in. But they will. He'll actually knock on the door, and put his face right up next to the glass, and kind of wall one eye at you, and give you this pitiful look, and whine. They think I'm mean to him because I won't let him in. But that's not it. I've never been mean to him, hell, I love him. It's just that I hate to see a dog manipulate people. So usually they all beg for him to come in and I finally say, All right, damn it, let the little spoiled turd in. Then he goes back to the boys' bedroom and gets in the bed with Billy Ray. Sleeps under the covers with him. It's pretty disgusting. MA will go in there in the morning and wake up Billy Ray, and he'll grunt, and Sam will grunt.

They'll do stuff like feed him ice cream and cookies, too. I swear he's just like a kid. You can't even enjoy a meal for him. He'll stand up on his hind legs and beg for whatever you're eating. Give you those mournful eyes. And finally he looks so pitiful and hungry you have to start feeding him off your plate or feel like a real bastard. He likes steak pretty well, shrimp, chicken. He'll eat lasagna. He'll eat just about anything out of your hand.

Billy Ray's got this big bluetick coon dog he got about six months ago, when he was still a pretty large puppy, pretty clumsy, real big feet and ears and all, and for a while Sam could knock him over and push him around, be a bully with him. He had the bluff on this puppy that weighed about forty pounds. He'd make out like he was going to eat his ass up, and the puppy would back off. Only now the coon dog's grown. A lot. Now he's hunting coons, and fighting them when he catches them. Wild coons. Which are like five handfuls of razor blades when they're fighting. The bluetick's named Jack. The only thing Sam can do to him now is try to bite his balls. That's about all he can reach. But the bluetick's going to get pissed off one of these days and probably bite his little nappy head off.

We roll through the door of the truck bay, our warning lights already revolving, flashing on the sidewalk and the big oaks along the street and the iron picket fence around the house across the street. The traffic stops for us and we turn left and head south down North Lamar, and Dwight stands on the siren and we pick up speed and race toward the first stop light a quarter mile away as the cars pull off to one side or I take the middle of the street and go around them, watching everything, watching the road, my speed, watching for people with their windows rolled up and the air conditioner going, or rock and roll turned up loud on their tape players, people who may not be able to hear me coming up behind them, people who might slam on their brakes. I never run a red light. Nobody with any sense driving a fire truck would run the red light at

North Lamar and Jefferson because you can't see anything coming either way down Jefferson until you are under the light. The siren hurts our ears but Dwight stands on it and we stop and look both ways at Jefferson and then go on through, up to the Square where the road splits and both sides of the street can get blocked on you if people slam on their brakes and then you have to make your own road, go around somebody. The sound of the siren bounces off the high buildings on the Square and amplifies itself and now that we have everybody's attention, we turn right and floor it down Jackson Avenue toward a boy who is strangling to death on his own blood this hot summer night.

We catch the next light on green and blow the air horn just in case and then we can see the blue lights of the city police cars and the red lights of the ambulance and we slow down and pull in and stop the pumper in the street, put the pump in gear, apply the parking brake. I pick up the radio mike and report that we're 10-7, engaged in an assignment, and then I report what we're looking at, which is a white Ford Pinto on the right-hand side of the street, pointed the wrong way and wrapped around a telephone pole at the edge of the sidewalk. Dwight is out and pulling on his coat and gloves. Harry arrives behind us in the rescue truck and parks. I hang up the mike and get out, pull on my gloves, get my helmet from the compartment, and walk over and look into the car. The passenger door is open and a nurse is in the front seat with a young man who is lying across the buckets, jammed tight against the shifter, covered with blood, his legs twisted behind him in the smashed remains of the driver's door. The nurse is jabbing a piece of surgical tubing down his throat, shouting, *Breathe,* baby, *breathe!*

Harry is getting the entry saw out of the rescue truck and I walk back to the pump panel and pull the lever that opens the booster line, a rubberized one-inch handline that's on a reel above the pump panel, and then I throttle the engine up and watch the pressure gauge until the needle sits steady on two hundred psi and then I walk off and leave it. Dwight pulls the line down with one hand and drags it over to the car and lays it down in the street. Harry is bringing the saw and I go back to where the nurse is working with the boy. She looks up at me and tells me that we've got to do something quick and I say, We'll do all we can, lady. The boy is trying to breathe and she has almost as much blood on her as he does. He probably has internal injuries, something ruptured in his chest, and she keeps saying that he's going to die before we can get him out. Here is this thing facing us again, this human and fragile thing called life wasting away before our eyes.

This is in the early eighties, before the city decided that we needed to spend seventy-five hundred dollars for a Hurst Tool, the Jaws of Life, and all we have is the Ram Tool, which I've already mentioned is not worth a shit in a situation like this, a wreck of this magnitude. It's only a hand-pumped hydraulic tool with various attachments. It has neither the power nor the speed. It won't pull a car apart like taffy the way the Hurst Tool will. All we've got is the

Ram Tool and the saw, so I walk around to the other side of the car where the door is bent into a U-shape against the telephone pole. For a moment I consider moving the car, calling a wrecker and yanking it off the pole, but then I tell Harry that we need to try and cut the door off. A whole lot of people are standing around watching us. I wish they'd all go away and let us do our work, but they're not about to do that. Hell no. This is too good to miss. They're going to stand right here and watch every fuckup we make.

Harry gets the saw cranked and noses the carbide blade into the door and a shower of orange sparks starts flying around in a circle. We keep the hose ready in case gasoline ignites and I already know this isn't going to work. The whole weight of the car is against the door and we won't get it off without cutting down the pole. It doesn't look possible to remove him. It doesn't look possible that the boy could have gotten himself into this kind of shape. It looks like he's going to die right here with all of us trying to prevent it.

I tell them to keep sawing and I go back around to the other side of the car where the nurse is screaming for the boy not to die, shouting things at me, I don't know what, I don't listen, I don't care what she's saying, I'm looking at this car and trying to figure some way to get the boy out of it as fast as I can. I lean over her with my flashlight and look at his legs. They're in that door behind him and the saw is running on the other side of the window, lighting up Harry's face and the safety goggles he has on. The boy breathes a little and then his breath catches in his chest and he makes that strangling noise again and she jabs the thing down his throat again. It's clogged with bubbles of air and blood and she keeps saying that we've got to do something, do something right now. She's about to get on my nerves and I wish to hell I did know what to do. I'm inside the car, crawling around, looking.

I get back out and look at the position of his body. And then I see it. He's got to come straight up. He's got to rise vertically out of that car like somebody levitating. The nurse tells me that they've got to call the rescue unit and I tell her, This is it, lady, this *is* the rescue unit and it's the only one you're going to get. I don't show her my First Responder patch, I don't tell her that I've been to the State Fire Academy to learn this shit, I don't tell her that if the city would open up its billfold I'd carve this car up like a Christmas turkey. I just go around to the other side and tell the guys who work with me to cut off the saw and let's get the windshield out.

We cover the nurse and the patient up with a blanket and then we take two fire axes and start chopping through the windshield, going around the edges, trying not to get glass splinters in our eyes, trying to remember to keep our face shields down. We go all the way around the top of the windshield and down both sides and then push it out over the hood and tear it loose from the gasket and throw it into the street like a dirty carpet. Then I'm up on the hood and reaching down through the hole for the shifter he's lodged against, that has his body hung. I push on it with all I have and it won't give. Somebody takes the blanket off the nurse and her patient and she's still working with him but he doesn't sound any better. I push against the shifter and it won't move. I say, Dwight, come here, help me. He crawls up beside me and lies down. I tell him that the boy is hung against the shifter, that we've got to bend it out of the way, but I'm not strong enough alone. I tell him to put his hand on mine on top of the shifter and he does. Dwight is a lot stronger than me and it starts to give. We push and strain, as hard as we can, and Dwight is nearly crushing my hand with his, but the shifter gives and bends over in the floor until it's away from him and not holding him anymore. Somebody has pushed the wheeled stretcher up near the car and we all reach and lift while somebody pulls traction on the patient, just in case he has a broken neck, and we slide the half-backboard in behind him and strap him to it and out he comes, onto the stretcher, the nurse walking beside him still jabbing the thing in and out of his throat, the respirator inside the ambulance only a few seconds away now, and they strap him down and load him up and get in with him and the doors slam and the ambulance screams down the street, the lonely wail of it washing over us as we stand and watch it go and listen to it fade away toward the hospital south of town.

I turn to Dwight and look at him. I'm glad he's so strong. I'm glad the boy didn't die. I understand why the nurse had no patience with us.

We roll up our shit and we go home. No thanks is needed from anybody. The city thanks us twice a month.

Now we are gathered in a little church in the woods, the yard of the church filled with muddy cars and muddy fire-trucks, and we have all driven up a muddy road and we are here to say our last goodbyes to Dwight, who lies in his coffin in front of the pulpit. He was strong, but he had high blood pressure, and he wasn't careful about taking his medicine, and two days ago, when he was rabbit hunting with his uncle and his cousin, he had either a stroke or a heart attack and died quickly in the woods, before they could get him some help. I have never been in a black church before, and of all the hundreds of people here, the faces of firefighters in their uniforms are the only white faces.

The church will not hold all the people who have come here. The church has no paint on the outside. I cannot believe that he is dead, but they open the coffin and there he lies, with his mustache, without the glasses he always wore, and a seventeen-year-old son bends over him with streaming eyes and kisses his cheek.

The preacher is standing at the pulpit, but the service is not going to begin until everybody is seated. All the pews are full and people are still coming in. The funeral procession looked miles long. Chairs are brought in and set down in the aisles and people sit in them, maybe forty or fifty more. We sit in silence, sweating in the heat, the women fanning themselves with little cardboard fans on wooden sticks, things I haven't seen or seen people use since I was a child in my own church and saw women do the same thing. The people stop coming in and somebody closes the door.

From a curtain behind the pulpit a line of old women come in wearing choir robes. There's maybe a dozen of them. They hold no hymnals in their hands and the organ sits dead and silent in the corner. The women sit down and put their hands in their laps and they begin singing. They begin singing like angels and they sing about Heaven and Jesus and the love of God, and the hair wants to go up on my neck because it is unearthly and beautiful and my ears love it like no singing I've ever heard, and the preacher stands tall in his black velvet robe with a face of stone and stares at the wall of the church. We sit enraptured and I look at the people in fine clothes, some still in work clothes, fresh from the job, all of us here for this wonderful music.

The singing ends. Then it begins again. I don't know how long it goes on. It stops again. It begins again. And finally it stops for good.

The preacher is a huge man. He looks like Alex Haley, only blacker. This man is as black as midnight. He begins his sermon in a gentle voice, talking of how we all must one day throw off this mortal coil, the way Dwight already has, that his suffering is over, that God's got a better world waiting. He talks of how he remembers Dwight in church as a child, how he saw him accept Jesus as his savior. He raises his voice a little and his words begin to assume a rhythm, and he starts to move, and we start to move a little with him. His voice gets louder and somebody says Amen. Somebody says, Yes, Lord. His voice rises to a higher pitch and I can see people swaying. It's going to be something. They start to shout and talk back to him and we keep quiet. There are two things going on here at one time. It's looking as if it's going to get out of hand. Pretty soon the preacher's moaning and his voice has gotten high and tight and he's caught up in it and the whole place is caught up in it and I'm caught up in it too and it's all I can do to keep from shouting something out at him myself because he's got me feeling something. The man's a great preacher and he's got all these people right in the palm of his hand and he's making them jump and move and yell, Yeah! Amen! Tell it, brother! Sweet Jesus! I close my eyes and feel it. It goes on and on and it's hot in the church and the little walls reverberate with sound until the preacher slows down like a clock unwinding and by then just about everybody's crying, me too, no more Dwight.

We carry the casket down a slippery hill, mud on the ladies' shoes, black and white people walking together to the muddy hole we're going to lower him into. We stand around while the preacher says his final words, while Dwight's wife cries and their children cry. We all have little boutonnieres in our lapels and we take them off and put them in a small pile on top of a wreath of flowers that is there. They lower the casket and it comes to rest six feet down. There is a large pile of streaked clay with five or six shovels stuck into it. Nobody tells us to, but the firefighters pick up the shovels and we start shoveling the clay over him. It's not even dirt. It will hardly fall off the shovel blade. Sometimes you have to shake it off. It lands in sticky clumps, sodden, wet, thumping loudly on his shiny casket. It takes a long time. We change positions, we pass the shovels around among us, we rest sometimes. It's not a pretty place to be buried. The land is of poor quality, with nothing but scrubby trees and weeds around. It's very hot. We keep shoveling. I'm off duty. And you can bet that I'm going to take my uniform shirt off and wear a clean T-shirt into Ireland's and sit down and have a very large drink when I get back to Oxford.

From here I can hear the coyotes screaming. They don't do it every night, but sometimes, usually late, after eleven p.m. or so, they'll start in. There's a big pack of them, a dozen at least, and they'll start howling and yipping, and all my neighbors' dogs will get to barking, and before long it's a hell of a racket and too loud to get any sleep.

I dug six little coyote pups out of an old culvert not a hundred yards from my house year before last. Billy Ray walked past the culvert and saw a pup stick its nose out of the culvert. He told me and I went up there and saw the same thing. It took me two days to dig them out. I could see them with a flashlight, all eyes and faces and fur, backed up in the darkness in there. The culvert was about twenty feet long, half full of dirt. It took me nearly a whole day just to chop it in two with an ax. Then I fashioned a long noose out of wire and a hoe handle and fished them out one at a time, patiently, slipping the noose over their heads, pulling them out. They never made a sound. No whine, no snarl, no growl. Absolutely silent. And when I'd finished I had six little wild things in the back of my pickup, their horrible little fangs already something to behold. They will kill and eat domestic dogs easily. For snacks. Hunting dogs. Hounds, German shepherds or poodles, doesn't matter. I always wondered what would happen if you put a pit bull and a wild coyote in the same pen. I would not be surprised if the pit bull fared poorly. Wild is a category of its own. Wild has strength, speed, a viciousness that tame can never possess.

The little coyote pups were nice in their own way. They couldn't have been over eight weeks old, yet they had the innate knowledge to be silent while I was roping them out. And they never offered to bite. At first I handled them with gloves, but there was no need. I'm glad to say that I didn't kill them, that I gave them to people who wanted to try and tame them. They didn't succeed. But we had six less coyotes in our pasture.

Sam will stand out in the yard and bark at them. But I hope he knows better than to go out there among them. He would be killed, and he would be eaten. And I would be a pretty sick boy.

I like to watch hawks. I like to watch them sail and flare over the pasture, set their wings, glide. Maybe I love them so much because they are so wild. Nothing touches a hawk, not fear, not compassion, nor weather, nor man. Man can catch them and work them, but never tame them. I love to see them sitting high in their trees with their wings folded, or galloping up on the wind until they gain enough speed to start soaring.

Around here, people used to shoot them all the time, until the government started protecting them. Now they've multiplied and it's easy to watch hawks work the fields and pastures near my home. I'd turn in any sorry son of a bitch I caught shooting a hawk. I'm not saying I'd turn in somebody for shooting a doe. It's not the same thing. I've shot does before, accidentally, twice. Both times there were bucks standing beside them. That shows you what a lousy shot I am. Although the meat is just as good.

Firefighters practice all the time. They're not always sitting in the house watching S and V on HBO. They're out in hot weather, testing their hose, laying it all out in the street with the nozzles closed and applying three hundred psi to it for five minutes to see that it won't burst, practicing forward and reverse lays, tying knots, studying all aspects of firefighting from their manuals. They drill and train and pre-plan attack strategies for various buildings, burn down condemned buildings, trying to get ready for the real thing when it comes, because it's going to come. They rappel off high structures, build fires in pits filled with flammable fuel, oil, Ketone, jet fuel, and then fight them. They lift weights and clean their equipment, check the pressure on their SCBAs, clean the masks, see that the regulators are functioning. They have to be as ready as they can be, but sometimes they can't be ready enough. Eventually they will run into something that no amount of training can prepare them for, because there are situations that are not covered in the books, things they cannot read about and learn how to handle, things that must be taken care of when they are encountered, in the dead of night, when most of the town lies sleeping, or at any hour, for that matter.

It's late, but I lie awake again in my bed at the main station, listening to the air conditioner blowing, the men snoring in the darkness around me, in total black and gloom, with the faint sound of cars passing on the street out front. A growing whine, a rising noise, the scream of tires skidding and a sudden WHUMP out there, then silence. I get out of bed quickly and run to the darkened day room, look out the window and see a car crumpled into the big oak directly across the street. I run back and turn on the lights, yell, put on my pants and boots, and some of us hurry across the street with flashlights and open the door of the car. A young man covered with blood has put his face through the windshield and then pulled it back, and he can't talk coherently not only because he is hurt so bad but also because he's so smashed on booze. He is trying to explain something, that this is a mistake, that he hasn't drunk that much, and his face is a horror movie too real to watch. We lay him in the street and wait for the ambulance. He covers his bloody face with his bloody hands, and he begins to cry. Cars slow down and stop, people begin to get out to see what has happened, why we are all kneeling in the street like this.

The call comes in around one a.m. Wayne Johnson Apartments are on fire. Out of sleep and into it again, full throttle, hard as we can go. The temperature is holding around five degrees. Will and I are working out of Station No. 3 and it's a short run, only about two blocks, and we roll up first and see in the yard a man on his back in front of the blazing apartment, fire leaping out the windows, the glass broken already, the flames lighting up the chairs and tables and cabinets melting and burning inside. The man on the ground is smoking. I don't mean smoking a cigarette. I mean the *man* is smoking.

We halt in front of the apartments, and I pause just long enough to put the pump in gear and apply the parking brake, then I get out and charge the booster line so that Will can start putting water on the fire. We can hear the sirens of the other trucks screaming as they come down the street to help us. Will takes the line off the truck and hits the fire, and I run to the man who is smoking.

I check his pulse and see that he is breathing, is not obviously burned, then go back to the pumper and climb up and take a wool blanket from behind the seat and go back to the man and wrap him in it. Then I go back to the truck and call headquarters and tell them what's happening, tell them to send an ambulance. The other trucks are in sight now, coming down the street, and I key the mike again and tell them to catch a plug on the way in and lay us a supply line. By now the fire is coming through the roof. You don't want it through the roof. You usually lose a building when a fire goes through the roof. The men from the other stations get out of their trucks and pull off hose lines and charge them. In just a few moments the fire breaks all the way through the roof. There is now a large yellow roaring hole. We open the nozzles, put up ladders and climb them, firing water down into the gigantic flames and the water goes everywhere and lands on us and freezes on our coats and helmets and gloves. We freeze on one side, burn on the other. We are illuminated in the light from the fire, bright flames dancing on the shiny red paint of the trucks where OXFORD FIRE DEPARTMENT is written in large gold letters. We scurry around like Santa's elves, the fire out of control, neighbors in their pajamas and housecoats and overcoats screaming for us to do something. And, well, ladies and gentlemen, looks like we're doing about all we can do. Maybe you'd like to get up here and man a hose for a while, let me get back in the truck and warm my hands and maybe smoke a cigarette? But this one whips us. The whole roof burns off before we can get it stopped. And by then we're so cold we don't really give a shit.

It turns out that the smoking man is drunk, and has set the apartment on fire over drunkenness and a woman, and has been pulled out by a neighbor, also drunk. We fuck around in the five-degree weather, in the water, for about three hours, long after the smoking man has been taken to the nice warm hospital in the nice warm ambulance. We don't even get our blanket back.

Lots of calls are in the middle of the night. Factory alarm systems go off. Cars burn. Fires start and go undetected because everybody is asleep. People get drunk and get in cars and hit somebody in the middle of the night. People set fires in dumpsters. In winter people try to thaw their frozen pipes with little hardware store propane torches and set their houses on fire. People put pennies behind the fuses in their fuseboxes and one night the wires can't stand it any longer. They let the batteries play out in their smoke detectors and don't replace them, or they spray hairspray all over their heads right beneath them, at God knows what hours, for God knows what reasons. They go off and leave chickens baking in their ovens at 450 degrees. (Nothing smells worse than a burnt chicken except a burnt human.) Gasoline tankers roll over. Cars leave the road and become airborne and center-punch trees. Old chimneys get cracks in them and fire runs between the brick and the wood. Old gas lines under houses leak, the gas pools and drifts until it finds a spark, WHOOM! People smoke in bed drunk and sober, doze off, wake to find their beds, their pajamas, and their rooms in flames. People burn their cars for insurance money, their homes for insurance money. They flush old gas from their service station tanks down the city's sewer system so that the fumes can run up a vent inside a grocery store and find a spark and blow part of the sewer system up. They do some really dumbass things, things that make a firefighter only shake his head, like thinking you wouldn't mind climbing an eighty-foot tree to get their cat down since you're not doing anything at the moment.

We're sitting in the day room of the fire station watching television one night, eating some things, drinking some coffee, talking, laughing. The fire phone rings and suddenly there is dead silence from us. Anderson, a new guy who is not from around here, picks up the fire phone and answers it, listens, smiles, then chuckles, then laughs, then hangs up the phone and continues to stare at the television.

Wally says, Well? Anderson just chuckles again. He never looks away from the television. He's really tickled by whatever he's just heard on the fire phone.

Some asshole on the phone, he says, still chuckling. Guy says, Ma name is Irvin Stepp and Ah live on Lizard Road and ma house is on far.

Chuckle.

Lizard Road. Like there's some place named that.

We sit frozen for a second. Anderson giggles again. Then the rest of us leap up and run and start getting our turnouts on and cranking the trucks because we know Irvin Stepp and where his house is on Lizard Road.

The truck is loaded with sticks of pulpwood and some of them are in the road and some are scattered in the ditch and some are actually inside the cab with the man. It is afternoon, summer, and there is no urgency to our work. The truck has come to rest nose down beside a high culvert, the back wheels almost resting on the road. Most of the load has shifted forward onto the cab, crushing the seat against the steering wheel, splintering the glass, pinning the doors. The sticks are pine, a foot in diameter or less, roughly five feet in length, and they were on their way to the pulpwood yard to be measured and bought.

The highway cops try to let some of the traffic through so that it doesn't get backed up any worse than it is. Accidents and stopped traffic on two-lane highways create other hazards, such as cars topping a hill and suddenly encountering a line of dead traffic. It makes the highway cops nervous and they try to keep the cars flowing if they can.

The ambulance is off to the side, the attendants waiting patiently with the wheeled stretcher. We are in and out of the cab with the man, trying to move things around, trying to shift some of the weight away from him. Some of the sticks are heavier than others and we move them as best we can. I am familiar with these fragrant, freshly-cut lengths of wood. They bring to mind the forest, shade, cool stands of timber, birds. Sometimes I cut pulpwood with my brother on my days off, felling the tall pines, eating lunch in the woods, sawing the trees up into five-foot lengths, hand-loading them onto my brother's one-ton truck, a truck about like this one.

After the wood has been moved, the easiest thing, the simplest thing, since the distance between the steering wheel and the seat is only a few inches, is to take the big four-foot boltcutters and spread the jaws wide over the rim of the wheel, and, using the strength of two men, bring the handles together to snap through the plastic coating and down to the metal ring that forms the base of the steering wheel and cut it in two, in two places. That removes the pressure and the man leans forward into what is left of it. Somebody will be getting a phone call, maybe already has.

Straining, heaving, careful not to slip against jagged metal or glass while working against the difficult slope of the ditch, we bring him out, the broken bone ends gently grating together, holding him hugged tightly to us, and we lay him in the short grass that borders the hot asphalt.

The public, as usual, is gathered to see, silent now, watchful, reverent for once in the face of death.

I try not to look at him but I do. As quickly as possible, we cover him with a sheet, because it is not decent to leave him exposed for all the world to see.

The eighteen-wheeler that pulled out in front of him idles on the left side of the highway, the driver shaken, crying, nauseated by what he has caused, realizing better than anybody on the scene the difficulty of stopping a loaded truck on a downhill grade.

The attendants come over with the stretcher and position it beside the white-wrapped bundle. All of us are sweating in the heat. The people stand watching, but I do not meet their eyes. I bend over the body and tuck the sheet around it tighter and then we bend and encircle him with our arms, four or five of us. It takes that many of us because he is so incredibly broken up, and we have to try to preserve a little of his human dignity.

The highway cops keep motioning for the cars to move through as we load him onto the stretcher. All faces look out windows as they creep by. The highway cops have sweated through their shirts. They want us to hurry up and get it over with.

The back doors of the ambulance are open and there is a chrome rail bolted to the floor of the ambulance and a locking jaw on the side of it. We lift the stretcher, push it into the back of the ambulance until it hits the channel that locks it straight, push it back, and then release it.

The doors slam shut. Both of the attendants will ride in front this trip. They get in, the front doors slam shut. The red light is on but they won't run the siren back to town. A radio squawks and we hear the transmission shift into gear. The cops wave goodbye to the attendants. The ambulance pulls off.

The cars continue to creep through, but soon the debris will be removed, thanks to us, and traffic will resume fifty-five miles per hour. The wrecker is approaching. We take off our gloves and one of my partners, who will die in an accident years later, opens the nozzle and drinks from the booster line. The water tank on the truck contains Tank-Savr, a rust inhibitor.

I tell him not to drink it, that it might kill him.

. . .

Screaming-ass burnout from Station No. 2, trailer fire at three-way intersection, lunch time, lunch on the table, rain, the road wet, be careful, watch it going around the curves. The trailer appears to be about half-destroyed when we get there (they always are), but our motivated nozzlemen knock the fire down and soon we're walking around inside, nobody killed, nobody burned, a family homeless for sure, though, and here's a dead puppy in the floor, a little brown thing, so sad, somebody's pet, I bet. Rick and Rob pick up the little wet dead animal and bring him outside to the scant light coming from the sky and we look at his eyes, glazed over, the evacuation of his bowels, sure signs of death, all right, but our van is there with the power saws and the halogen lights and the ropes and rappelling gear and the oxygen and Rick says, Let's give him a shot.

A couple of people light cigarettes, shake their heads, Shit, that fucking dog's *dead,* Rick, but he and Rob get the oxygen cylinder out and crack the valve open and slide the tube into the puppy's mouth and leave it in for a little bit and the glaze starts to come off his eyes. Hey, check this, we say, and gather around. His ribs rise and fall one time. Big Rick sits there on the linoleum in the floor of the van, cradling the puppy on his lap, stroking him a little, still wearing his turnouts and his OFD cap, and the puppy makes some noise halfway between a bark and a yelp, blows smoke out like he's been enjoying a Marlboro, then takes another breath. Dead, huh? Rick says, and a little crowd starts to form. Rob sits there grinning and chewing his gum. He was going fishing but then it rained and then this happened. Pretty soon the puppy's making all kinds of yelping noises and trying to raise his head, howling like the oldest ghost in the world, and we figure he's reliving the fire.

You done come back to the world, boy, we tell him.

Poot Man and I are standing at the window of Fire Station No. 3 one pretty Sunday morning and see a young man without a shirt walking down the side of the bridge that faces the station. The young man is jumping and waving his arms, shouting. I open the window and as he gets closer it's easy to hear that he's screaming about nine hundred kinds of *motherfuckers!* into the peaceful, church-worshipping, happy spring morning. What's the matter with that fucker? Poot Man wants to know. I believe the sumbitch is crazy, I say. We watch him come closer, and he picks up a Coke bottle off the road. A car with two boys in it pulls up at the stop sign by the station, directly across from the young man now armed with a Coke bottle.

He's fixing to put that Coke bottle right through their windshield, I say. But he doesn't. He just throws it to the road at his feet and it shatters into bits. He leaps and screams, waving his arms. We can't imagine what he's so pissed off about. I hope he don't come over here, Poot Man says. Maybe we ought to get away from this window, I say. And then I see the cop car coming down the street, fast, lights off. Looka there, I say.

The young crazy man sees the police about the same time we do and it gives him pause. The car slows and swings in and stops about twenty feet from him, and a cop I know named Bob gets out from the passenger side, holding what looks like a nickel-plated Colt .45 near his hip, not showing the gun, moving in a half-crouch. I hear him say: You get your ass on the ground. The young man kneels as Bob comes closer. Hands on your head, Bob says. The young man obeys, and he looks like a prisoner of war. He starts crying, saying something about his brother. Bob holsters the gun and cuffs him. The young man is now awfully cooperative and polite. Bob puts him into the back seat. There's nothing quite like a good cop when you need one.

It grieves me deep in my heart now to have to write about the death of Sam. He died while I was staying overnight at the University of Notre Dame, where I had gone to give a reading. He was involved in two fights with a black chow over a bitch that was in heat. He was hurt badly in the first fight, and did not survive the second one.

Only a few days before I left for South Bend, I had noticed that he was running with a little cocker spaniel one of my neighbors owned. I figured she was in heat and this turned out to be the case. I was driving by one day and Sam was there, and he trotted out into the road to meet me. I told him to stay out of the road, and to get his little ass home after a while. I knew he was happy, because he looked happy, and I knew he was probably finally at long last getting himself a little from the cocker spaniel, so I was happy for him.

But on Saturday afternoon, the kids brought him home pretty chewed up. His throat was wet from where the chow had mauled him, and he was all hunched up, and he stank. He just kind of stood there in the carport in a little miserable drawn-up ball, shivering. He looked really bad, but I never thought of taking him to the vet. He'd been in fights before and had healed up okay. I told the kids to put him in the pen and not let him out. He smelled too bad to stay in the house.

I had an early flight out of Memphis the next morning, and Mary Annie took me up there like she always does. She couldn't go to the gate with me because of the terrorist threat and tighter security while the Gulf War was being fought, so we had to say goodbye in the terminal. I got to South Bend late in the afternoon, and had just forty-five minutes to take a shower and be ready to go to dinner with some people and then give my reading. There was a party afterward, like there always is, and it was nearly midnight when I got back to my hotel on the campus. A couple of kids from the university walked up just as I was about to go in, and wanted to talk some more, so I invited them up to my room for a drink.

My thoughts were more on home than anything else as I talked to these kids. The place I was in held no importance to me other than the money it brought me. I felt sometimes that I was just a whore with a high price. I could be had,

I'd do my gig and jump through my hoops, but you had to come up with a check and some plane tickets. Otherwise I'd stay home.

I never went to college, and I felt alien on college campuses. All I had done was stay in a room for ten years and write. I felt that I was ill-equipped to spout any advice to fledgling writers, and I liked critiquing their manuscripts even less. There was always something so terrible, so bad, written by somebody who had no idea what a story was supposed to be about, that it would be nearly impossible to find anything good to say about it. I didn't like that part of it. What I liked was standing before a couple of hundred people and reading one of my stories and watching what happened to them. That night I had a new one, a long one, one that I had worked on for nearly a year, one that had taken nearly an hour to read, and I was about talked out.

The students finally left. I probably hastened their departure by starting to pour them Cokes instead of whiskey and Cokes, by giving the gentle hint that the hour was late and I was tired. I had probably given them more of my time than they had hoped for. I wished them good luck with their work.

Next morning I went down to the dining room and had a huge breakfast by myself, then lingered over my coffee and cigarettes. I love my coffee and cigarettes, although I'm certainly aware of how bad smoking is for you. My body is getting older and I can feel the ravages of time much sharper now than I could twenty years ago. I wouldn't be happy if I couldn't smoke, because I would always want something I couldn't have. It's the same way with drinking. I've seen many people damaged by drinking and I still see them, and I know the evils of it, having tasted them myself many times.

Most all the trouble I was ever in was caused by drinking, whether it was trouble with the law or fights or whatever, because whiskey twists my head and I need to stay away from it unless there's somebody around who can take care of me, but there's nothing more enjoyable to me than to get into my truck late on a summer evening and ride down the road for an hour or so, drinking a beer, looking out at the fields and the warm horizon where the sun has just gone down, listening to Otis Redding or ZZ Top or Leonard Cohen, and watching the road go by. I love the land I was born to and I never tire of seeing the seasons and the weather change over it, or the hawks that sit high in the trees, or the rabbits that bound across the road, or the coons that band together in spring when they're rutting, or later at night, the owls that swoop low across the ditches or fly down to light in the road in front of you with mice caught in their talons, owls that glare at you with a hateful look before gathering their prey and swooping back up into a black and rainy night on their huge beating wings.

I finished my coffee, went back to my room and called MA's office, and found out that she and Shane had been in a wreck and had been taken to the hospital. Everything fell apart in that minute. I tried to hold myself together, but all I could find out was that they had been in a wreck and had been taken to the hospital by ambulance. My mind blanked out and I couldn't think of any of the phone numbers I needed. I tried to call my mother and she was gone. I tried to call MA's mother and she was gone. Both of them gone to the hospital, I knew. I couldn't even remember the fire station numbers. The only number I could think of was Square Books in Oxford, so I called Richard Howorth, told him where I was and what had happened and gave him my number, and asked him to find out what he could and then call me back. Then I sat down beside the phone to wait.

It was a terrible time, that waiting. I couldn't drive it out of my mind that one of them or maybe both of them were dead. All those dead in the highways I'd seen, the bodies I'd pulled from cars. I knew that was the wrong thing to think, and I sat there and willed the phone to ring. It did. It was Richard, saying he had talked to a nurse at the hospital who was reluctant to give him any information, always a bad sign. He gave me the number of the hospital, and I called, and was eventually connected to my brother who was there waiting, and he told me that MA and Shane were bruised up some, but not seriously hurt.

It was nearly time to meet with my class, but I had other plans. I took my bags downstairs and told the group waiting for me about what had happened, and asked them to get me to the airport as soon as they could. I had a ticket for a flight at three o'clock, and I wanted to exchange it for an earlier flight if I could.

I missed a United flight by five minutes and couldn't buy a ticket for a Northwest flight that was already overbooked. What I had to do was hold onto the ticket I had and wait for the three o'clock flight. I spent most of the time in a bar drinking whiskey and making phone calls. I finally got ahold of MA and talked to her for a while. Her chest was badly bruised, and Shane had come out of his seatbelt and hit the windshield and had a big knot on his head, but they had no cuts, no broken bones. She promised that they were all right, and then she said there was something she had to tell me. That's when she told me that Sam was dead. He had gotten out of the pen and gone down and fought the chow again.

She had taken him to Dr. Harlan, our vet, and he had put Sam on a table and shaved his neck to expose the dozen big cuts in his throat, and had done all he could do for him. She said the whole time she moved around the room as the vet did his work, Sam kept his eyes on her, and she said he seemed to be pleading with his eyes, seemed to be trying to say, Please help me. Then he died.

Maybe the whiskey made me cry in a public place, in an airport in South Bend, Indiana, with people watching, with snow falling. Maybe I was so overcome with relief that they were all right that I couldn't take the extra load of losing him. I knew that I was still over six hours away from home, and those six hours had to be gone through and lived through and there wasn't any way to shorten them.

They went somewhere. I went through them. Richard

picked me up at the airport in Memphis and at eight-thirty that night I walked into my house. I even missed the funeral. Billy Ray had already buried him under a good tree in the pasture. He wouldn't speak of him then, and he won't speak of him now.

It's cold in the woods. I sit up high in a tree and the sun rises incredibly slowly from the woods behind me and my feet are frozen in my boots and my hands are rigid with cold on the rifle.

Squirrels play on the ground below me. They run up and down the trees and a hunting owl sails over and they hide themselves underneath limbs until the owl passes. I watch these things and shiver in my tree. I want a system that makes it easier, something like a deer locator that clips onto your belt and lets you know when one's close by so you can get ready, so you don't have to sit every second without moving and freezing your ass off. I begin to doubt that there are even any deer in these woods, although the scrape I have built my stand close to has huge hoofprints and wet soil where one has soaked it with his urine, and pawed the ground, and torn a bush into shreds with his horns.

But he is not going to come by and check to see if a doe in heat has visited his scrape. He is huge and he is old and he knows when the season opens because he has lived long enough to know that when the weather cools and he hears the sound of truck engines and Honda engines in the woods, the men are out looking for him, and he has found some small hidden place to lie during the daylight hours, some little clump of bushes where nobody would ever think of looking for him, and he will only rise out of it when the sun goes down and the men in the woods are gone. Maybe he has been shot before. Maybe he was downed and leaped away to safety and healed up and learned. He has been here. His tracks and his urine and the torn bushes where he has scraped the velvet away from his itching horns prove it, but he is not here now, just me.

I climb down. My feet are so dead to me that I can't feel them, and I build a small fire on the ground some distance away from my stand, finding a pine knot and peeling orange shavings of wood from it, laying them under small sticks and larger sticks and lighting them and warming my hands over the fire as I squat and shiver and wait for the sun to come up. It never rises any slower than when you are sitting in a tree waiting for it to warm you.

I drink the last of my cold coffee. I smoke a cigarette. And I pull my boots back on, my socks steaming from the fire, and put the Marlin on half-cock and ease my way through the woods. I move maybe a quarter mile an hour, probably less. I stand and listen and look. Old tortoise shells in the woods, dead and white. Piles of deer-sign still wet and fresh. I bend and touch them. The huge oaks and the ground beneath them raked nearly clean by the deer hooves for the acorns that are there. I've seen the squirrels walk between their legs in years past, all of them feeding together, not disturbing each other, a fine thing to be able to witness. The deer probably watch me as I go along. They live in these woods and I don't. I am only an intruder, come to try and kill them in their home.

The morning stays cold. I walk slowly. I stop often, stand still, look and listen. I watch for movement, do the same thing they do. I cross a little sand road and ease into the young pines bordering it and my feet are quiet on the wet needles. I see other scrapes, other bushes hooked and torn. They are here. They have vast amounts of patience. They will stand still and let me walk by. I move into the wind.

The sun comes up and I stop on a steep hillside where I can see up into a big hollow of hardwood trees with a little creek running down through the bottom of it. It's so easy to get discouraged. Lay all these plans. Get up two hours before daylight, fix your breakfast, everybody else asleep in the house, Mary Annie and the two little boys, Billy Ray five and Shane just born barely, sprawled sleeping in the bed. Coffee in the kitchen, pulling your hunting knife from the scabbard and testing the edge above the remains of your eggs to see that it is sharp.

Move on up through the woods and see that there is nothing moving in the hollow, time to sit down and take a break, smoke a cigarette, rest.

The ground is wet and frozen and my ass is wet. I sit smoking the cigarette, the rifle across my lap. In the creek below me I see yellow horns move and I drop the cigarette from my fingers and look at him. He is standing there, testing the wind with his nose. The white patch of his throat, his tail down, not alarmed at all. I count the six points on his head and raise the rifle out of my lap in extra–slow motion and move it toward my shoulder as he swings his rack, as he stands in the creek in his world and doesn't know that I am here. I don't look into his black eyes. That would alarm him and he'd run. The sun is out and it's ten-thirty as I lay the crosshairs on his chest. I nestle my eye into the scope, and small bushes with dead leaves garnish the bright patch of white hair that runs all the way up from his belly. I pull the hammer back to full cock. I want to kill him dead, with one shot. He's the most beautiful thing I've ever seen besides my babies. The crosshairs rest steady on his chest and I try to calm myself. I'm reminded of the days at Parris Island, when they told us to get steady and then squeeze off, not to dread the slap of the rifle. I hold it firmly and touch the trigger gently, fire, clap of sound, slap of the rifle all instantaneous, and he goes down. He kicks hard in the leaves. I lever another round into the chamber and hold it on his chest again. He is kicking violently on the ground, thrashing in the leaves. But I don't believe that he'll get up. I don't want to shoot him again. It's hurt me bad enough to shoot him the first time.

In less than ten seconds the thrashing dies down. I hold the scope on him and look. Jesus Christ. I've killed him. He lies dead.

I ease the hammer back down into half-cock and I go down to him. He lies in a bright patch of sunshine on the brown leaves with brilliant red blood leaking out of the hole in his chest where the 170-grain Winchester bullet has gone in and scrambled his lungs and heart. His head lies propped up by the antlers, his eyes growing glassy and dull, fading from their former gleam.

I unload the rifle first, jacking all the rounds out of the magazine and the one in the chamber, emptying it completely so that it's safe and no threat. I lay it aside, prop it on a log. I sit down beside him and feel the long hairs on his coat. I stroke the brownish-gray pelt. I note the nest of white hairs on his belly, and look at the horns. He's the biggest one I've ever killed. He suffered some. But he didn't suffer a lot. He felt confusion and then died. Not unlike Sam, years later. Would that we could all do that when it comes.

I pull my knife out. I turn him over onto his back. I cut the testicles off, and then I enter his body cavity with the blade, running it between two spread fingers to keep from cutting into the guts, and run it all the way up to his chest, where the ridge of bone between his ribs stops the knife. I hack through the cartilage and open him up to his throat, and then I go back down to the hindquarters and carefully cut around the anus and draw it out with my fist and tie it off with a strip of cloth I cut off my shirt. It would be easier if I had somebody to help me, but I don't mind doing it by myself. There is no sound but the wind in the trees while I do these necessary things on my knees. The diaphragm holds the respiratory organs away from the digestive organs and I slice through it with the Schrade. I reach far up into the throat and sever the windpipe and haul forth the guts and organs and pull them out. I dip water from the creek with my cap and wash out the body cavity. He's field dressed. I wash my bloody hands.

I sit down and look at him and smoke another cigarette. The day has warmed and it's a little after eleven. I finish the cigarette and shoulder the rifle, and take him by one horn. I start pulling him.

We go down hillsides and up other hillsides and I estimate his weight at 150 pounds, a big deer for Mississippi. The horn is hard in my hand and it hurts and I have to stop often to rest. I get hot and I start coming out of my clothes. The temperature is probably nearing fifty degrees. I keep pulling him and pulling him and I take off all the clothes I can and sling them over my shoulder and still they are not enough. My heart starts pounding. It beats harder than it has ever beat before. I stop and we lie in the dead leaves together. I put my finger on my wrist and look at my watch and measure my pulse at 130 beats a minute. I rest, pull some more, rest some more, pull some more, holding the rifle and my clothes, the flies starting to buzz on him, and I drag him up over the last hill and up to my father-in-law's '67 Chevy pickup, and put the rifle inside, checking it again to see that it's unloaded, and then I strain everything I have to get the deer into the back end, and then I drive out of the road that leads to Vallis Chapel, a little church deep in the woods where services were once held, where once I walked among the silent pews and saw a wasp nest that spanned twenty inches and a small owl that stood on a ledge and saw me and spread his small brown wings to glide without sound into the summer brightness, and was gone.

I took the deer home and we took pictures of him. There is one that remains, me in my cowboy boots holding the deer's head up by the horns, two little puppies that later died of parvo prancing around him, my hair down in my face, a much younger guy than I am now. That's been ten or eleven years ago. And I haven't killed another deer since then. Some people probably wouldn't think of these things as nearly a religious experience. But I felt God in my trigger finger that day, in the way he lifted his horns and tested the wind, trying to smell and see me, where I was sitting so still and small against that little tree, smoking a cigarette, almost ready to go home.

I see these people going through the dumpsters. I can see their heads sticking out of the dumpsters long before I get there with my bags of trash. Usually when I see people with their heads sticking out of the dumpsters, I just keep on driving by, come back later. If you stop, they'll be hungry for your Coke and beer cans, and will want to know if you have any, and if you do, they'll request that you deposit them in the back end of their pickups instead of inside the dumpster.

Item: A man and his wife who live down on old Highway 7 can be seen regularly in the afternoons trudging up the hill to the dumpsters above their house, him with his plastic sack over his shoulder, her in shorts, always looking either a little lost or a little ready to be insulted that you know what she's doing. They have a medium-nice brick home. Neither of them seems to be disabled. She stands outside the dumpster patiently while he paws through it, patiently pawing through the shit. They seem to go there every day, like milkmen, maybe mailmen.

Item: I go over to the dumpsters one evening with some trash and a bicycle that one of my children has discarded. Some black people are over there, fishing in the river, hanging around the dumpsters. Some small children are with them, beautiful little children in torn shorts and dirty T-shirts. Many little tiny pigtails tied with white yarn in the little girls' hair. I lift the old bicycle over my head when I bring it out of the truck. There's not much wrong with it. The chain is rusted solid and it has a flat tire. Other than that it's probably rideable. I start to throw it into the dumpster and one of the ladies says, Mister? Mister. I stop. You going to throw that bike away? she says. Yeah, I say. I look at her. I'm still holding it over my head. They look fearful, shy. You want it? I say. You don't want it? she says. I set it on the ground. The children are all looking at it. They are staring hard, but making no sound. The bike is small, a child's model, and it was blue once but is now rusted and blue. Maybe it was LeAnne's. Maybe it was Shane's. The mother comes up and I offer the bicycle out to her and lean it over to her and she takes it and looks it over. There really ain't much wrong with it, I say. It needs that flat fixed. Needs a little oil on that chain. You could spray you a little WD-40 on it and it'd probably break right loose. Yessir, she says. We'll sure take it. The children come up then, oohing and aahing. They retreat in a small group with their mother, touching the bike, talking to each other in soft voices, nodding, approving, starting to smile.

We are trained to save lives, and we try to. We take a CPR course once a year, every year. An officer from the Oxford Police Department comes over to teach us and we get down on the floor with a dummy from Sweden or somewhere named Resuci-Annie and practice on her, clear her airway, practice one-man and two-man CPR, do it on a baby dummy, too, except it doesn't have a name, we just call it Baby Dummy.

We learn the Heimlich Maneuver, which makes folks blow their steak out, and we make jokes about it. We go to the First Responder course at the State Fire Academy and learn everything from extrication to checking blood pressure to delivering babies. You never know if you'll ever need any of this stuff or not.

. . .

Item: Shane Brown, about four years old, swallows a piece of steak at Dino's Pizza Parlor and stops talking and claws at his throat. I jerk him out of his seat and turn him upside down over my arm, hitting him hard between the shoulder blades, trying to dislodge the meat. It won't come out. I have him hanging there, shaking him, gawkers in the restaurant be damned. I keep whacking him between the shoulder blades and finally he spits the piece of meat out. Small disturbance, and we sit back down to our meal.

Item: LeAnne Brown, about five years old, swallows a big grape at my mother's kitchen table, stops talking, and begins clawing at her throat. I snatch her up, turn her upside down, and start hitting her between the shoulder blades. She coughs and gags but it won't come out. Drool spins from her mouth. I keep hitting her and it won't come out. She starts to go limp in my arms and still it won't come out. I run my finger into her throat to try and sweep her airway but it's lodged in her throat. I don't want to kill her hitting her, trying to save her life. I hang her back upside down and keep hitting her between the shoulder blades, and everybody's starting to scream. I don't know what I'm saying, but I'm saying something, maybe praying out loud, maybe not. She coughs and the grape drops to the floor and rolls. In a minute she's all right. Eat more careful, baby, I say.

. . .

Item: Mary Annie Brown, about thirty years old, eating steak in the kitchen at Mamaw's house, stops talking and starts clawing at her throat, then suddenly leaps up and runs out on the back porch, me right behind her. She stops beside a post and puts one hand on it, bent over from the waist, waving her arms and hands, saying nothing. I come up behind her and make a fist with my right hand and put it against her stomach just below her ribs and close my other hand over it and give her a hard sharp squeeze. The chunk of steak blows out of her mouth and lands in the darkness of the yard. She turns around and we lean on each other for a moment. She waves her hand in front of her face again.

Eat more careful, baby.

Item: One of our captains is in a Sizzlin' Steakhouse in Tupelo and a lady's baby starts choking on something. The lady stands up and starts screaming, shaking the baby, going hysterical because the baby has stopped breathing. The captain gets up from his meal and crosses the room and takes the baby away from her, hanging it over his arm, whacking it gently between the shoulder blades. Whatever is in the baby's throat comes out, and the woman snatches the baby back and runs out of the restaurant without a word.

Item: Some of the boys on another shift, just playing around out of boredom and in good-natured fun, tie one of the nozzlemen into a rolling chair with lots of rope and push him off down Price Hill into traffic. They say his screams are something to behold.

Item: We get a call to a house down on the south end of town, evidently on fire, but when we arrive, lay out hose, hook to the hydrant, and force the door, the house is not burning. The house has *been* burning, as evidenced by the traces of black smoke that have stained the soffit boards and cornices. Inside, the house is cold. The owners are gone and a chair backed with thick upholstery has been left in front of an electric heater that kicked on and ignited the chair, which eventually smoldered out.

A fire must have three things: heat, fuel, and oxygen. Remove any one of these things and the fire will go out. The house was tight, and once the fire got underway and started burning, it consumed and depleted the available oxygen and smothered itself out. Not much damage, but there have been casualties. Inside the tub in the bathroom, just behind the shower curtain, Johnny and I find two dead cats.

Them sumbitches deadern *hell,* Cap'n Brown, Johnny says. I agree. We smoke a cigarette and look around. Just like we've been taught, the principles of fire science do work, as evidenced by this fire going from the incipient, or beginning stage, then to the free-burning stage, and then to the smoldering stage and then going out when no fresh supply of oxygen was introduced.

Unfortunately, the owners soon arrive, sometime after we've checked the whole house to make sure there are no pockets of fire hiding anywhere. It's very simple how it happened as we recreate it: the heater kicked on, the chair caught fire and filled the house with smoke, the cats sought escape in the bathtub as they always do, and were killed by smoke inhalation before the fire could smother itself out. Open and shut case. We feel a little like detectives. The only thing now is having to go out in the front yard and tell the owners that their pets didn't make it.

The lady is already weeping in the yard. She can see that her house hasn't burned down. But she keeps hollering about her *babies,* wanting to know if her *babies* are okay. We're going to have to be tactful, we're going to have to let this woman down as gently as we can, try to break it to her kindly. The woman is wringing her hands as Johnny and I come out. I think Johnny has his sunglasses on.

Oh, the lady says. Oh, what about my *babies?*

Sorry, lady, Johnny says. They dead.

I used to work with a great firefighter named Ted. We worked for about three years out of Station No. 3, and he was about as good as they come. But he had actually begun service with the city as an ambulance attendant. Years before we were firefighters together, Ted and his crew had been called one day to a farm outside of town to free a man whose private parts had been entangled in a gasoline-engine post-hole digger. When Ted got back, he said that the man had been in terrible shape, his clothes caught and twisted by the auger that drills the holes. I don't remember how they got him loose, probably cut most of his clothes off or something, but at any rate they rescued his equipment and the man was extremely relieved and grateful.

When they got back to the main station, somebody from *The Oxford Eagle*, our local paper, called to get the daily run report, and Ted was trying to explain the nature of the run they'd just returned from. I was sitting there listening to him.

Ted was and is a very polite man. Rarely cusses. He was also the middleweight boxing champion of the Third Fleet when he was a corporal in the Marine Corps. And he was trying to get across to this reporter in a tactful way what had happened out there.

Well, Ted said, his, uh, his . . . uh, *scrotum* was caught in this post-hole digger.

Evidently the person on the phone didn't understand and asked again.

Well, Ted said, his, uh, his . . . uh, *testicles* was caught in this post-hole digger.

And still the person on the phone didn't get it.

His *balls!* Ted said.

My *kitty* died. I reckon it got up under Billy Ray's truck and sat on the spare tire and then jumped off at some point during the time I backed out of the drive and drove 2.1 miles down the road and turned left and then went 3.4 miles and turned left again, and then went about a mile and a half and stopped.

Coming back I saw a little yellow kitty in the road dead with a bloody head and I said, Shit, surely that ain't it. Got back over to the house and there wasn't a kitty around. Not a little yellow one that size and color, nor any other color. So I drove back over there. It was him. Or her. I never had determined his/her sex. It was all my fault and I felt pretty bad about it, since I'd hated and loved cats all my life and always thought that one day I'd find the one that was right for me.

I stopped in the road and took a good look at it. It was it, all right. Head all bloody. Over the course of the past several hours the cars going up and down the road had shifted its little body back and forth across the centerline and by late evening it was only a little scrap of orange fur, like it had never had any bones or anything. I started to stop and scoop it up but I didn't. Not since the damage was already done. I'd been afraid something like this was going to happen, but I didn't know what to do about it. It was already to the point where I had taken to leaning out the door of the truck and working the clutch and brake with my head below the frame, looking to make sure none of them were under there, and they usually were. I'd had to coax several of them out from under the truck a few times before I could back out of the carport. Now it had happened to one and could happen again and there didn't seem to be any remedy to it. Just raise cats up and murder them by accident. The thing about it was that puppies would never get in that kind of shape. That may be why I've always preferred dogs whenever I've had a choice.

I took off there and made a little round through the country. I felt pretty dismayed about the whole thing but I also felt that if they just wouldn't get up under the truck and sit on the spare tire, they wouldn't have to make the choice of whether or not to jump out from under it while it was going sixty mph.

I figured what happened was that it was a matter of attrition. He sat up under there while I cranked the truck up and maybe got a little nervous, thought maybe *well something's happening here but I don't know if it's bad enough to jump out from under it right now or not,* then I backed out of the carport and started down the driveway and dust started whirling up under the truck and gravel flying and he said maybe *well this thing's picking up speed and it looks like maybe I ought to jump,* but then sometimes cars are not coming from either direction and I just swing out into the road and pick up a little more speed and he thinks maybe *well you done messed up now, it's going faster all the time and now there's some black stuff going by underneath with yellow stripes and it's too late to jump so let's just hang on and see if it ever slows down and then maybe I'll jump,* but then I start shifting up into third and fourth and am usually drinking a beer by then or trying to find something decent on the radio or tapes in the glove box and I'm not thinking about a cat hitching a ride with me on a Michelin radial. The cat's thinking *oh shit* by then or *this damn thing ain't slowing down so maybe I just better hang on for dear life,* and that goes on for three or four miles. If I stop at the dump he's got a chance to get off then, if he just would; if he'd let me know he's under there I'd pick him up and put him in the cab with me and let him walk over my shoulders and across the back of the seats, but he's probably dizzy and disoriented and by the time he's had time to think about it I've slung the garbage over my shoulder and thrown it into the dumpster and we're rolling again, highballing it up the Hartsfield Hill, running in fifth gear, picking up speed for the ridges. He doesn't want to get off then for sure but about another mile is the place he evidently picks, and I don't even notice him, rolling across the pavement, through my rearview mirror. I'm listening to Clint Black or somebody, trying to light a cigarette. I'm trying to get over here and pump some water out of my pond at Tula, man, I'm busy. I've got to get some dozer work done if the water ever goes down. I don't have time to ponder a bunch of kitty cats.

But I get over to Tula and everything is peaceful and placid. When I get there I know why Thoreau went where he did. I think someday I might write a book called *On Miss Lutee's Pond.* It would be about the peace and tranquillity that's available at the little house I own over there and it would be about the mangy hairless hound dog with half a tail that I found sleeping on one of my beds in that house after I left a window up and it would be about my neighbor coming over there one deadly hot August afternoon while I was up on the roof trying to put some paint on it and him telling a long and awful story about this terrible car wreck he saw one time. It would be about how nice it is to sit out on the front porch when the sun is going down and drink a glass of whiskey. It would be about owning a piece of land where the pines are tall and the cedars are thick and the ticks are thick. It would be about petting a giant black bull that lives in my pasture and not shooting the turtles because they want to live, too, and the eight-and-a-half-pound catfish I caught back in March while my brother was telling me a story about two guys going fishing, Frank and Kenny, about how Kenny hurried home from work and his wife had a big supper laid out for him but he didn't have time to eat, told his wife, Honey I just got time for a bite, I mean she had fried green tomatoes and pork chops and boiled okra in the peas, he just leaned over and got a bite here and there, telling her he had to get his fishing pole and meet Frank right away. They were supposed to meet at the store in fifteen minutes. He loaded up all his stuff, his wife mad at him because he didn't eat all the good supper she'd fixed for him, and got down to the store, no Frank. Where in the hell's Frank? Sat around there ten or fifteen minutes, no Frank, where in the hell's Frank? Waited and waited and finally decided to drive back to his house and call Frank, Frank, where in the hell you at? Kenny, I'm just now getting my stuff together, I had to eat supper, I'll be down there in five minutes, take it easy, calm down. Kenny rushes back to the store, no Frank, where in the hell's Frank. Sits around, no Frank. Frank drives up. Frank, where in the hell you been? Kenny's mad already. Kenny can't position his fishing pole in the window so Frank has to do it for him. Kenny has to sit in the back seat because his pole's in the front seat. They drive on over to the lake and the sun's going down, they don't have much time to fish, don't catch anything, Kenny gets in a real bad mood. Here he's done waited on Frank all evening and missed his good supper and ain't caught shit. Sun goes down and it's time to go home. Frank done screwed up Kenny's whole evening. They start walking out and Kenny gets madder and madder, thinking about how Frank's done messed up his whole day. They're walking over a bunch of big rocks, and Kenny decides he'll pick up a big rock and just kill Frank, just crush his damn head. He picks up a big stone with both hands and staggers up behind Frank, holding it up over his head, just waiting for Frank to turn around so he can drop it on his head. Frank turns around and sticks a cocked .38 pistol up Kenny's left nostril and says, What you gonna do now, Kenny? Kenny drops the rock and says, I don't know, Frank, something came over me, I just lost my head. Frank takes the .38 out of Kenny's nostril and they ride back on home together, and about that time that big catfish comes up and swallows my minnow and the pole bends double and my brother yells, You gonna lose him! and I yell, Hell I can't hold him! and mud splashes everywhere and I drag him up close to the bank and the hook comes out of his mouth and I leap in the water and grab him behind the gills and duckwalk him up the bank and my brother says, Boy, I thought you's gonna lose him.

Late that night I get back home and not just one kitty is gone but all three kitties are gone and the mama cat is walking around in the carport looking anxious. Where are they? I look up under the truck but they're not up under there. LeAnne's going to have a fit when she finds out they're gone because she spends a lot of time playing with them on the couch and holding them up to her face and hugging them and all.

I get back in the truck even though it's three a.m. and I ride back over that way, the road deserted, decent people in bed asleep everywhere. I get back to within a quarter mile of where the flattened kitty is and there are two kitties huddled on the side of the road. I slam on the brakes and get out and they come to me when I squat down beside the ditch saying, Kitty kitty kitty, and I scoop them up and get back in the truck and put them on the seat and go on down the road. They're crying loud, scared to death, walking around on the tops of the seats and behind my neck and over my shoulders as I turn around at the Rock Ridge Colored Church and then drive back by the flattened kitty, their brother maybe, or maybe their sister, and go home with them. Their mama meets them when I let them out of the truck.

Later Shane wants to know where the yellow kitty is and I say I don't know. He says, You sure, Dad? and I say, Sure I'm sure, and he says, You sure, Dad? and looks at me and I see that I'm not fooling him, because he's a kid you can't kid much, but I'm backing out of the driveway going somewhere and I just keep on backing and go on down the drive.

Back in the old days, when we're still furnishing fire protection for the county, we get a call one afternoon that a house is on fire near Taylor, a little community about ten miles south of town. The bad thing about running fire service for the county out of the city is the time involved in traveling to a structure that's on fire. Time is of essence in stopping a fire, and that's why we always try to get there as fast as we can, within the margins of safety. Driving to anything in the county is hazardous because you're traveling at a higher rate of speed, often on two-lane blacktop roads, sometimes dirt roads, sometimes mud roads. Sometimes you have to take your pumper across wooden bridges that don't look strong enough to hold it up.

This house is up some pig trail, and once we leave the blacktop, the way is directed by people standing along the little drive pointing their fingers. It's early in my career and I don't know much, but I know when we roll up that there's no saving this house. The entire structure is blazing from top to bottom, and it has started falling in. We pull the hoses off anyway, and start pumping out of our 750-gallon booster tank. Hot isn't the word for it. This thing will burn your ass off even through your turnouts. We go up to it and start putting water on it, but this doesn't even faze the flames. Nearly instantly, we notice a pretty bad thing: the 250-gallon LP-gas tank that furnishes heat for the house has heated cherry red. It's sitting less than twenty feet from the house, and if it blows we'll all be burnt to death, blown to Kingdom Come, to Jesus or whoever's waiting for us. There's only one thing to do: put a stream of water on it. I get that job, and I kneel and turn to it, open the nozzle, and the water sizzles with a terrible ferocity when it hits it. But I'm being burned by the heat from the house at my back. I've never been hotter in my life. My hands are burning, my neck, my head, my back and legs and arms. Somebody shouts something, and suddenly a hose is turned on me. I'm putting a stream on the tank and they're putting a stream on me. I stay where I am even though I don't want to. I'm cooling the tank if the fire from the house doesn't get me first. I'm drowning in the water and burning at the same time. I have to close my eyes and just endure it. It's bad, but this is my job, and I can't run from it, much as I'd like to. The only thing that consoles me is knowing that we'll eventually run out of water and be forced to retreat.

I don't know how long it lasts. The red cherry glow on the tank starts to vanish. The house caves in with a great roar of flames. My partners put more water on that side of the house and finally they tell me I can move. I stand up and everybody looks at me and asks me if I'm all right. They can see what I can't. They lead me away from the tank and they tell me to get that stuff off. They start unbuckling my coat fast and they pull it off me. They hold it up in front of me so that I can see what I'm wearing. The whole back of the coat is gone, nothing left but two hanging wings of charred black canvas with pockets. They tell me to take my helmet off and look at it. I do that and hold it in my hands. The top of it is bubbled up and blistered, melted.

They just grin and shake their heads. I'm not grinning a whole lot.

Cookout. The whole department. Fishing, drinking beer, water skiing, or boatriding anyway since it's only March, out at Sardis Lake north of town. We're going to cook a pig but first we have to kill the pig. Captain Louie and I, a lowly nozzleman, arrive at the pigpen for the execution at the designated time and look at the pig, who is pink and grunting in curiosity with his nose lifted as we stand outside the pen and study him. We've all been laying these plans for weeks. We're going to haul our boats and our campers and our camping equipment and tents and Coleman stoves and barbecue grills out to the lake along with our sleeping bags and spend the whole damn weekend out there, sleeping under the stars, having a good time. The people who are on duty today will come out as soon as their shifts are over. It's going to be really fine. But first we have to shoot this pig.

Louie hands me a loaded Ruger .22, a nice little semi-automatic pistol. It's heavy in my hand. The pig grunts and walks up to the wire of the pen. He seems friendly. If he were a dog he'd be wagging his tail.

This pig's not that big. He's probably what's commonly known as a shoat hog, a young boar that hasn't had his nuts cut out with a sharp knife yet.

All right, Brown, Louie says. Shoot the sumbitch right between the eyes. He's standing there drawing hard on a cigarette, one hand on his hip, ready to get this over with so we can dress the pig. We're in charge of getting the pig.

I point the pistol at the pig. He's looking all around, sniffing at the air. He thinks we've come to feed him something, maybe. I hold the sights right between his eyes—what if I shoot him in the eye?—but he weaves his head around and the gun waves around in my hand as I follow his head.

He's looking right at me, I say.

Hold your head still, you son of a bitch, Louie says. But the pig keeps moving around, grunting, oinking, making the noises pigs do.

I can't do it, man, I say, and I lower the pistol.

Gimme that damn gun, he says, and snatches the pistol away from me. In a blinding movement that doesn't seem to allow for the possibility of aiming, he slips the safety and pops the pig dead square between the eyes. The pig screams and keels over, all four legs stiff, quivering on the ground, dead as a hammer.

Captain Louie unloads the pistol and sticks it in his

pocket and bends the wire of the pen down and straddles it, telling me to come on and help him, a little disgusted with me, I can tell.

You ever steam-cleaned a hog? Louie says, as he cranks up the steam cleaner at his father-in-law's combination wrecker yard/auto repair/used furniture store. You can buy fireworks here, too. The pig is lying across the tailgate of Louie's GMC pickup, a little blood running down his nose. Louie explains that it ought to work, hell, all you do when you scald one at home is pour scalding water on him and scrape the hair off with a knife. You know this steam is as hot as scalding water, he says. It makes sense to me.

Louie puts the steam to the hog and I pick up a knife and start scraping the hog, and sure enough, the hair starts coming off, softened by the steam. We'll have this sumbitch slick as a baby's ass in no time, he says. People stand watching us at our work.

We pull into the back parking lot of the main fire station with the pig and everybody who's on duty is out there waiting for us. The campout is going to start this afternoon but first we've got to gut the pig, clean the pig, get him ready for the fire we're going to build under him. Everybody's all excited and wishing they weren't on duty. It's like a fever that's consumed everybody. Springtime is coming and we want to be out with Nature. They'll come out in the morning after they get off. The ones who are camping out tonight and are due on duty in the morning will come back in. It's a campout in shifts, B-C, C-A, A-B, but everybody is included, wives, kids, everybody.

We let the tailgate down and willing hands reach in for the pig as we start telling them how we steam-cleaned him. The pig is indeed pink and smooth as a baby's butt. We carry the pig over to the back door of the fire station and lay him down as knives are pulled out of pockets.

Rob is on duty and running the shift and everybody's offering advice as to the gutting of the pig. Damn, I wish I wasn't on duty, Rob says. He squats down beside the pig and pinches up one of the nipples on its belly.

You've heard the expression, Useless as tits on a boar hog? he says.

By the time we get the pig gutted and loaded back into the pickup, he's told us about fifty times that he wishes he wasn't on duty.

Here we are. Out at the lake. Some people have already arrived. Barbecue grills have already been set up and fired up. Hillbilly is on the way with a couple of gallons of barbecue sauce that a friend of his who works for the food services department at Ole Miss has mixed up. There are plenty of shade trees, no leaves yet, true, but we're camping right beside the lake.

Damn, ain't this fine? we all say. We have to have a conference about how to cook the pig. Some say bury it in coals. Some say cut it up and cook it on a grill. What we finally decide to do is dig a hole and fill it with burning wood, and build a spit to put the pig on, and turn him slowly over the fire while slathering him with barbecue sauce all night. It sounds like a good idea and we get to work, gathering wood, digging the hole, finding two forked trees to cut down to hold the spit. Some of us are already drinking beer. A lot of us, actually.

I have to leave sometime to go get MA, who is pretty pregnant but still up for a good camping trip like this, and besides, all the other wives are coming, too.

We dig, cut, pile wood, and Hillbilly arrives with the barbecue sauce. By now it's afternoon and more people are coming in. It's beginning to look like a parking lot, with all the vehicles and boats and campers. It's going to be *so* damn fine.

Late in the afternoon I get back with MA and we all put the pig on the spit, wire him to it with coat hangers, and we light the fire. Everybody agrees to take turns turning the pig all night and putting the sauce on him.

Before long it starts getting dark. We're having a hell of a good time. We cook hamburgers, hot dogs, chicken, even some rabbit. Captain Louie has a large rabbit-raising operation. This is several months before I get into the rabbit-raising business myself, from which I never fully recover, because you have to kill the rabbits just like you do pigs, but I won't get into that yet.

Word comes that Rob has called everybody in the department who's off duty and has finally found somebody who's agreed to work his shift for him tonight, and he'll be out here shortly.

Even Uncle Bunky has showed up. He has a snort behind his car once in a while, comes back to the fire.

We're squatting around the fire, talking, laughing. It's wonderful. The pig looks great, dead and barbecue sauce all over his head. We're using a little mop to slap the sauce on him and we're turning him every once in a while. We know it's going to take all night, but everybody's willing to help. Everybody's willing to give up some sleep for the common good, for the common barbecue.

Rob arrives pretty soon with a case of Miller Lite. We squat around the fire talking. It's colder than we expected. It's pretty damned frigid as a matter of fact, and people are gathered around their campfires. I don't spend much time with MA. I'm pretty much staying with this pig.

Later in the night, lots of people have gone to sleep. MA is asleep. Most of the wives are asleep. Actually there are very few people up. Rob gets up once in a while to get another Lite.

Hillbilly and I squat beside the fire, looking at each other and looking at the pig.

Later, much later, maybe around two or three in the morning, Rob and Hillbilly and I are the only ones still up. Everybody else has crawled into their nice warm vans and campers and cars and trucks and gone to sleep. Rob stands up, drains his last Lite, and says, Throw the sumbitch in the lake or burn him up, I'm going to sleep. He disappears into the night and Hillbilly and I look at each other.

For the rest of the night, freezing on one side and burning on the other, Hillbilly and I turn the pig and put the sauce on him, not saying much, just waiting for dawn, which rises about a week later, pale and cold across the lake. Captain Louie's wife gets up, comes to the fire, yawns, puts coffee on for us. A blessed soul if there ever was one. She gives us a cup and we're glad to have it.

When daylight comes, Hillbilly hands me a knife and I slice into the meat and remove a small piece and chew it. That piece is good, done. But then I slice deeper and it's raw, soured, and we look at each other. The whole pig has ruined. We should have used charcoal instead of wood. We really messed up. We stagger to our beds and sleep a little. Later we throw the pig into the woods. Rob gets his Jeep mired in mud trying to launch my ski boat, and the lake is muddy, choppy with big waves. People get seasick. People start leaving early. A cold wind comes up and it's not a nice day. Before long almost everybody is gone. MA and I go back to our home, a house trailer in a pasture, and go to sleep, glad that it's over.

Item: It is a cold January day, and we stand at dawn on a barren hill in Calhoun County and hold our dibbles over the fire, warming the handles, until David tells us to go ahead and hit it. We load the bags with baby pines and strap them around our waists and we move off in a group, the sky gray like steel and one solid color. A snow sky. The iron dibble has a blade four inches wide, a foot long, with a little step built into it that you kick with your heel to drive it into the ground. The men to my left and right are eight feet away. We dig the hole with the dibble, bend and put the pine tree in it, stick the dibble in the ground behind it, push it forward to close the hole around it, twist it, pull out the dibble, kick the hole with the heel, move forward six feet, bend again.

The wind is blowing and it freezes our hands through

our gloves. We don't speak. We are on something like a plateau and the hills for many miles away are open to us. It is cold and sad. Our day has just begun.

After a while it starts snowing, big wet flakes that fall soundlessly on our shoulders and melt. It falls thicker and faster and the landscape starts turning white. The hills in the distance are removed and we keep moving forward. We are far from the truck. The black men around me are dark ghosts moving through the snow. Then we hear the faint sound of the horn on David's truck. He is calling. Calling us back.

Later in the morning, I sit on the couch in David's trailer, drinking straight vodka from the bottle and chasing it with a canned Coke. He doesn't have any orange juice or tomato juice or grapefruit juice to mix it with, so we just do it this way. Pat Coleman is here with us. He works with us sometimes.

Outside it's still snowing. We go to the door once in a while and look out to a familiar land now white and strange.

Pat and David caution me to go easy on the vodka. They don't care for me drinking their booze, they just think it might make me drunk. When I don't pay any attention to them, they just grin.

By ten o'clock, I've had about as much as I can stand. I stop drinking, stand up, tell them I need to go home. They ask me if I'll be all right. I tell them I will. I thank them for the drinks and go outside.

The black truck is a 1953 Chevrolet with no heater, no radio, one taillight, and it came from the factory like that. MA's grandfather bought it when it was brand new. It has a straight six with a shift on the column, a high-speeded rear end, and sixteen-inch tires.

I don't slide off the road in the snow. I go home, to Mamaw's house. We live in the house with her now, and I move from room to room looking for a place to write. At this point I've written a couple of novels and close to a hundred short stories in this house and not much of all that is any good. I am wondering if it ever will be, if the rejection slips will ever stop coming, how much longer it will take to learn what I want to learn. The most frightening thing to think is that it might never come, but I never allow myself to think about that very much. I just tell myself that I have to keep trying, that what I want is worth the price I'm paying.

But I don't write anything today. I go inside and lie down on the floor with all my clothes on, a pillow under my head, my cap over my face, and I stay there, sleeping off the vodka for the rest of the day.

Item: Winter, cold, dark. Bringing wood in from the stacked lengths in the yard, red oak, mostly, some pin oak and white oak mixed in, but the red splits easiest. I buy a full load off a pulpwood truck from Harris Talley, a gigantic gentle black man, whose little children get up on the truck with him, his wife, too, and unload it in the yard. I saw it up with my Stihl 041 and split it.

The house is filled with the smell of woodsmoke. A good smell, a solid heat. Shane is around eighteen months old, Billy Ray about five, LeAnne not born or even conceived yet.

I work at a place called Comanche Pottery on my days off from the fire department. It's a few miles out from the north end of town. I go in at eight and get off at five, one hour for lunch, which I spend listening to music in my car, and eating the lunch MA has packed for me.

We pour liquid plaster into molds of different shapes, flower pots, Indian heads, leopards, elephants. We dip them in a wax solution to seal them from the weather and the elements. We package them with a machine that wraps hot plastic around them, then we load them into trucks.

Some of the people who work at this place are from Haven House, a home out near Old Sardis Road for recovering alcoholics and drug addicts, people who have come to the end of their road and are trying to get a new start. None of them stay long. They drift on out into their lives, maybe even back into their drugs and alcohol.

While I work I think of the things I'll try to write when I get home. And now I am home, in the kitchen, supper finished, MA and the boys up in the front room watching television, trying to let me alone, let me work, let me write. I sit at the typewriter, a new Smith-Corona that I will type on until it is completely useless, until the keys don't work, until the return carriage slips.

I'm writing something about a family of people walking down a road with their possessions in their hands, homeless people, fruit pickers, laborers, an old man, his wife, a boy, two girls. I know that it is the beginning of another novel, and in my mind I begin to call it *Nomads*. But later I will call it *Joe*.

I have chosen this thing to do, away from my family, the doors closed, characters who form in my head and move to the paper, black symbols on a white sheet, no more than that. It may seem senseless to anybody else, but I know there is a purpose to my work: the spending of years at the typewriter writing until I become better than I am now, until I can publish a book, until I can see that book in a library or a bookstore.

I love this thing, even if it does not love back.

It's never any trouble finding a wreck we're sent to because everybody else is already there, the Highway Patrol, the ambulances. It has to be so bad that nobody else can do anything before they call us. We're kind of like the last resort. The attendants will have already made their initial survey and determined that the patient cannot be removed without the extrication tool, the Jaws of Life. Traffic will often be blocked, the pulsing red and blue lights visible from a great distance.

This accident is about two miles south of the city limits. A late model New Yorker is thirty yards off the right-hand side of the highway, the driver's door almost up against a tree, the result of a head-on collision. The other car is beside the road, broken glass scattered, but either there are no victims to be extricated or they have already been taken to the hospital by another ambulance.

Everybody knows what to do. Canvas has to be laid out, lights set up, blocks, chains, the gasoline engine unit that furnishes the hydraulic power for the Hurst Tool, and the tool itself. Thirty-foot hoses have to be connected from the power unit to the tool, the unit cranked, a careful examination of the patient made, and then we begin. He is in a great amount of pain and his legs are trapped. The tree is not blocking the door and we force it open, pop the pins top and bottom and the door falls off. Getting his legs out will be harder. The dashboard has moved back and down onto him, and we'll have to do what's known as a dash roll, where everything, including the steering wheel and the steering column, is pulled forward and up to free him. It's going to take some time, and our patient is hurting. The one thing we must not do is hurt him any worse.

One of the things we do first that is nearly standard procedure is to remove most of the roof. We take out the windshield, fasten the shears to the jaws of the tool, and then make four cuts: one on each windshield post, and two in the roof, back behind the driver's seat, on each side. This allows us to lift the roof up in one piece and flip it back on itself, so that we have an open area to work in, so that we can step right up into the car. We've got to be in there to look at things or run the tool from in there.

One of the things on the car that's not going to move

much when we apply the incredible force of the Hurst Tool to it is the frame. And the biggest piece of steel inside the car that's connected to the dashboard is the steering column. We fasten chains to the frame and the steering column. Some stuff will break, fly out under pressure and maybe kill the patient, so you hook to something strong. We run the chains up from the front of the frame, over the front bumper, across the hood. We run the other set of chains, once we've wrapped them around the column, across the dash where the windshield used to be and across the hood to meet the other set of chains. But we don't join the chains. We leave maybe a foot and a half of space between them, and then spread the jaws of the tool open that far. All we have to do is hook the chains to the tool with steel pins, start closing the jaws, and then watch and listen to the immense tearing of metal and the steady crunching of plastic and aluminum and rubber and whatever else the dash is composed of as the steering column begins to rise up and split it all in two.

We can also roll the dash up from the floor. We can place solid oak blocks beneath the car, things that won't give like the floor of the car will give, spread the jaws between the dash and the floor enough to get a "bite" in some metal, and push it up.

In this wreck, we have to do both. Sometimes in collisions everything moves back and down, and things get terribly smashed, and this is what has happened here. It's not long before we have him out, but he tears off a cervical collar once we have him strapped onto the stretcher, and complains about the strap across his chest until the attendants remove it. It's only when they get him to the hospital and take X rays that they find out he has multiple broken ribs.

Once our patient is gone, our job is nearly over. A pumper always accompanies us to furnish tools or water or manpower, and sometimes to clean up. The troopers have discretion on this; if they want their highway washed down, we charge a line and put a man on it, sweeping the broken glass and debris into the ditches and roadside grass with the force of the water.

We pack up all our equipment, our protective blankets for the patient, the lights, the chains, the shears, the blocks, the gasoline unit, the tool, the canvas, everything we unloaded, put the line back on the reel on the pumper, turn around in the road while the troopers halt traffic for us, lights flashing, then turn the lights off and head back to town to refuel and check equipment. Elapsed time: thirty furious minutes running on adrenaline.

Captain Louie didn't coerce me into the rabbit-raising operation. It was done strictly of my own volition after I looked at his, which I thought was supreme cool. All his bunnies were in hutches with self-feeders and self-waterers, under a shady shed with big fans blowing cool air through wet feed sacks in to them so they wouldn't get too hot. It was summer then, and he explained everything to me.

It took about twenty-one days for a mama rabbit to have her babies. You put a wooden box in there with her and she pulled hair out of her chest and built a nest, and the babies got born, and not long after they were born you bred her again, which only took a few moments after you put the daddy rabbit in there with her. He mounted her almost immediately, hunched her very rapidly a few times, fell off and lay on his side and drummed a hind foot on the floor of the cage—evidently because it was so good for him—and then you took him out. In eight weeks you butchered or sold those young bunnies—they'd dress out at two pounds of meat—and the whole process repeated itself at regular intervals. Captain Louie had hundreds of them. He was selling the shit out of them at two dollars apiece. I bought two does and a buck as fast as I could pull the money out of my pocket and stuck them in the trunk of my car and went home to start building my own hutches, ready for the dollars to roll in.

Nothing much happened at first. It took a while to figure out that I had two does in the same cage together. I hadn't seen any sex going on so I just threw all three of them in the cage together and things got taken care of real quick.

I'd built my hutches out of two-by-fours, half-inch wire mesh sides and floors, and plywood tops. We were still living out in the pasture then, and I noticed that the grass grew a lot thicker and greener under the rabbit hutches. All that good Purina Rabbit Chow I was buying from Leslie Stewart at the feed mill by the fifty-pound bag got sent through those rabbits pretty fast. But I took the fertilizer they made and put it on my tomatoes that year and I'd never raised such pretty ones. Boy, boy, I said to myself. Look at the added benefits.

It wasn't long before one of my rabbits, a black-and-white one, went funny. She started hopping and leaping, and kind of screaming, inside her cage. I didn't know what was wrong but I knew it was time for her to have her babies and I told MA that I was going to bring her inside the trailer and put her in the bathtub and watch her, which I did. I sat on top of the commode lid and watched her for a long time. She did some more screaming and jumping around in there, and then she died. I could hardly believe it. I took her out into the yard and performed a Caesarean section on her with a sharp knife, by flashlight, and discovered eight little well-formed rabbits, nearly hairless, ears tucked down slick on their heads, all encased in their tiny amniotic sacs, waiting to be born, and dead, my little black-and-white mama rabbit dead, too. Bad omen, nine dead rabbits instead of nine live ones.

We took it hard. I can't remember if MA was pregnant with BR or if he was already born. But I do know that one morning not long after that, MA screamed and came running in the back door of the trailer, saying that there was something in the cage with the other mama rabbit, something awful. I went out and looked and there were five little tiny pink hairless baby rabbits mewling and looking for a tit. I saw that things were going to work out and I bought a few more bucks and does so we wouldn't be committing incest.

Well, as these things do, it got to the uneasy stage, and I've written about this in some of my fiction. The rabbits grew up, and got to be eight weeks old, and it came time to knock them in the head, and butcher them. Oh, I did it. I did it for a good long while. I'd do it and try not to think too much about it. I'd use a hammer handle or something.

You'd have to pick them up by the hind legs and hit them hard, and then they were just dead meat, something to be dressed, not unlike a coon or a squirrel or a deer you'd shot out in the woods. I dressed them, skinned them, cut them up and fried them, and they were sure good. All the boys at the fire station raved about how good it was whenever I fried up a big skillet of rabbit and made some gravy to go over it, but they just didn't know what I was going through at home.

I was seeing those little rabbits born. Children were petting them. To kill them, I'd have to pick some time when children weren't around, and then have to tell the kids that the cage door had gotten open and they'd run away. I had to hide the evidence of my crimes, and I began to devise new ways of murdering them. Sometimes I shot them.

Before long I began to realize that I was raising these soft gentle creatures, who had harmed no person or animal, with the express purpose of killing them, and if this continued, the blood of hundreds of animals was going to be upon my hands. In an unbelievably short amount of time, as I culled out does from litters for future brood does, they had outgrown the small hutches I'd originally built, and I was forced to move the whole tribe to an abandoned farmhouse on my father-in-law's place, lock the door, and just dump their feed in, grab rabbits once in a while, kill them, or have them bred, bring water, sweep and pick up their shit, throw bales of hay in for them to nest in, little rabbit heads poking out of every rat hole and crevice in the house.

But one day a day came. I was taking yet *another* fifty-pound bag of Purina Rabbit Chow out to the old farmhouse and I stepped inside, and there they were: little rabbits hopping all over the place. You couldn't walk for them. They weren't wild or frightened. I could pick up any of them. I was never once bitten. I could stroke that silky fur. And I said to myself: You cannot do this anymore. So I opened the door. Opened it wide. I started whooping, and yelling, and kicking the walls, and I ran every rabbit in that house out into the pasture, sixty-one acres of the finest pastureland in Lafayette County, a fact admitted to by my agriculture teacher and FFA advisor in high school.

Those rabbits were brown rabbits, black rabbits, white rabbits, black-and-white rabbits with white noses, brown-and-white rabbits with white noses. I knew they'd run wild and breed with the cottontails on our place.

I was glad to be done with it. I felt like the hit man who grows sick after too many deaths.

Years and years later, Sam would sometimes catch a small one in the garden, bring it proudly back to me, lay it at my feet. It would look like a cottontail, but often as not it would have a white nose.

New Year's Day, 1989: we are called to a house just off Access Road, a cold morning, the wind bitter and freezing. We catch the plug going in and lay line far down a dirt driveway that many other houses share. The house at the end of the drive is blazing away, and maybe twenty or thirty people are standing in the yard, crying and holding on to each other. Wally and some of the other guys knock most of the fire down but there are still pockets of fire here and there. We mop up small fires, take furniture out into the yard and onto the porch, trying to salvage some of it, but the inside of the house has been demolished, complete sections of wall between rooms burned away, most of the whole rear of the house gone, smoke and fire lingering and holding in corners, licking in the rafters of the roof, smoldering behind the siding. This house is ruined. I don't know if it can be rebuilt. I don't know if they have insurance.

We spend about an hour and a half there, until we're sure everything is out, that it isn't going to rekindle once we get back to the station. We pull everything apart that might hide fire, go through every room over and over again. There is no sense leaving if we're going to have to come back. We're cold and muddy, covered with ashes and soot, our faces black and grime-streaked. Wally is in charge and it's his decision as to when to take up. Finally we get the order and we shut everything down and start draining and rolling up the muddy hose.

It's only as I'm nearly ready to get into Engine 4 and start backing down the driveway that I find out that this is a gathering of one family to celebrate New Year's Day, that some of them have come from other states for this celebration. I look at the people again, their home destroyed, one child burned and gone to the hospital, all the possessions in the house ruined or saturated with smoke and water. What can anybody say to them?

You learn early to go in low, that heat and smoke rise into the ceiling, that cooler air is near the floor. You learn to button your collar tightly around your neck, to pull the gauntlets of your gloves up over the cuffs of your coat, that embers can go anywhere skin is exposed. You learn that you are only human flesh, not Superman, and that you can burn like a candle.

You try to go easy on the air that's inside the tank on your back, try to be calm and not overly exert yourself, try and save some of your strength. You learn about exhaustion and giving it all you've got, then having to reach back and pull up some more. Suck it up and go.

You learn eventually not to let your legs tremble when you're pressing hard on the gas or the diesel pedal, when you're driving into something that is unknown.

One day if you make rank you will be promoted to driver or pump operator or lieutenant and you will discover what it feels like to roll up to a burning structure, a house that somebody lives in, or a university dormitory where hundreds of people live, or a business upon whose commerce somebody's livelihood depends. You will change in that moment, stop being a nozzleman and become instead the operator of the apparatus the nozzlemen are pulling lines from, and you will know then that the knowledge pushed into your head at dry training sessions in the fire station must now be applied to practical use, quickly, with no mistakes, because there are men you know whose lives are going to depend on a steady supply of water, at the right pressure, for as long as it takes to put the fire out.

And on that first time you'll probably be like I was, scared shitless. But you can't let that stop you from doing your job.

You learn the difficulty of raising a ladder and pulling the rope and raising the extensions up to a second-floor window, and the difficulty of climbing that ladder with a charged inch-and-a-half line and then opening it and staying on the ladder without falling.

You learn of ropes and safety belts, insulated gloves to move downed high-voltage lines, nozzle pressure and friction loss and the rule of thumb for a two-and-a-half-inch nozzle. You learn to check the flow pressure on a fire hydrant and what burning plastic tastes like, the way it will make you gag and cough and puke when those fumes get into your lungs and you know that something very bad has come inside your body. You see death and hear the sounds of the injured. Some days you look at the fire phone and have a bad feeling, smoke more cigarettes, glance at the phone, and sometimes it rings. Sometimes you're wrong and the night passes without trouble.

You learn to love a job that is not like sacking groceries or working in a factory or painting houses, because everybody watches you when you come down the street. You wear a blue uniform with silver or brass or gold, and you get free day-old doughnuts from the bakery shop down the street. At Christmas people bring in pies, cakes, cookies, ham, smoked sausage, cheese, half-pints of whiskey. They thank you for your work in a season of good cheer. One freezing December night the whole department gathers with eighty steaks and Wally parks his wheeled cooker and dumps in sixty or seventy pounds of charcoal to cook them and you have drinks and play Bingo for prizes that businesses in your town have donated, a rechargeable flashlight from the auto supply, a hot-air popcorn popper from a department store, a case of beer from the grocery down the street.

You lay out hose in the deadly summer heat on a street with no shade, hook it all up, hundreds and hundreds of feet of it, put closed nozzles on the end of the hose, and run the pressure up to three hundred psi and hold it for five minutes. If a piece bursts and creates a waterstorm on the street, you remove that section from the line and throw it away. Then you shut it down and drain it and write down the identification number of every piece of hose that survived the test and put it all back on the truck, thirteen hundred feet of it, and you make new bends and turns so the rubber coating inside it won't kink and start to dry-rot.

You learn the major arteries of the body and the names of the bones and how to splint a leg or an arm, how to tie off and cut an umbilical cord. You learn to read blood pressure, administer oxygen. You see amounts of blood that are unbelievable, not realizing until it's actually spilled how much the human body holds. You crawl up under taxpayers' houses for their dogs, go inside culverts where snakes may be hiding for their cats. You learn to do whatever is called for.

No two days are ever the same and you're thankful for that. You dread the winter and the advent of ice. On an August day you pray that the city will behave and let you lie under the air conditioner and read a good book, draw easy money.

You learn that your muscles and bones and tendons get older and that you cannot remain forever young. You test the pump on the truck every day when you come on duty, make sure it's full of fuel, clean, full of water, that the extinguishers are up. You check that your turnouts are all together, hanging on the hook that has your name written above it, and that both your gloves are in your coat pocket. You make sure your flashlight works. You test the siren and the lights because everything has to be in readiness. You shut it all down and stand back and look at the deep red Imron paint, the gold leafing and lettering, the chrome valves and caps, the shiny chains and levers, the fluid-filled pressure gauges, the beds filled with woven nylon, the nozzles folded back into layers of hose, the hydrant wrenches snug in their holders, everything on this magnificent machine. You learn every inch of your truck and you know which compartments hold the forcible entry tools, the exhaust fans for removing smoke from a house, the power saws, the portable generator, the pike poles, the scoops, the salvage covers, the boltcutters, the axes, the ropes, the rappelling gear. You look at all of it over and over again and then you go inside the fire station and get a cup of coffee, sit down with a magazine or a newspaper, and once more, you wait for whatever comes your way.

The house called Rowan Oak is the home of William Faulkner and it has a very sophisticated fire alarm system. It is sensitive enough that a bug can walk inside it and set it off, but still the trucks have to roll. Rowan Oak is a landmark and thousands of visitors come to Oxford every year to walk the grounds, peer into the rooms inside the house, look at a pair of his shoes still sitting beside a bed on the second floor.

I had never gone there until sometime in the late seventies when a film crew from New York was shooting something, probably a documentary, in the yard and wanted some rain, only there was no rain that day. Ted and I were called out to improvise for these people. Rowan Oak has its very own fire plug sitting there in the yard.

If two houses are sitting close together and one of them

catches on fire, it can generate enough heat to catch the neighboring house on fire. You combat that with a stream of water on the other house to keep it cool while you're putting the first house out, or by setting up something called a water curtain. It's basically a hose cap with a narrow slot cut into it. You lay out a line and put the water curtain on the end of it instead of a nozzle, and charge the line, and it throws up a wall of water to protect the exposed house.

Ted and I went over to Rowan Oak, hooked a line to the plug, put a water curtain on the end of it, and the New Yorkers had their rain. While we were waiting on them to get through, I took a good first look at Rowan Oak.

It's a big house, two full stories, wide and deep and white. Large columns on the front run all the way up to the second-story gallery. All the windows have green shutters, and it's in pretty good shape for a house that's a hundred and fifty years old.

It's easy to forget that you're inside a city when you're standing in Mr. Faulkner's yard. The noise of traffic is muted, and the big cedars that line the drive leading to the house tower up and form a cool shade. Most of what you can see from the yard is woods. You can't see University Avenue, with all its gas stations and fast-food joints, and you can't see South Lamar, with all its wonderful old homes and huge trees, but you can see Mr. Faulkner's barn where he kept the horses, and the pasture fence that penned them in, and the old cookhouse out back where rabbits sit in the grass.

I like to walk around the old wooden fence, and look at the trees, and think about what he did with his life. I figure he didn't pay much attention to what the world thought. He just went on and wrote his novels and stories and eventually won the Nobel Prize. I was born in this town, still live here, but it's something to stand in that yard, maybe a block from where I'm sitting now, and think about that, about all those novels and stories that came from inside that house. I know a guy who used to caddy for him and his brother, John. He said John always tipped and William never would. Mrs. Faye Bland told me he used to come in The Mansion, a restaurant where she was a waitress, and drink a cup of coffee every night, leave a dime tip. Said he wore an old shabby coat with patches on the elbows; said, Larry, to look at him you'd think he didn't have nothing.

But he had something.

This is New York City, fall, 1989. Coming in on the plane I looked out the window and saw the harbor and the Statue of Liberty and the hundreds of tiny white dots in the water that were sailboats tacking in the wind and beyond all that the great gray city, too big to believe, filled with life on streets I would soon have to walk.

All my hours have paid off now, all my little meaningless rejection slips mean something now, my first novel, *Dirty Work,* is out and I'm going on *The Today Show* to talk about it. All the boys at the fire station will be watching, all my relatives, anybody from home who knows me and knows this is happening.

I don't want to be here. I resisted it for a long time. I thought they wouldn't be able to understand my accent, and I was afraid I would make a mistake on live television.

To me this place is vastly fascinating and fearsome. You read about all the killings, all the drugs and guns and meanness. You read books like *Report From Engine Co. 82* by Dennis Smith and then when you get on these streets you see those men come down them in their pumpers, trying to get through the incredible network of traffic, and it looks like they'll never make it to wherever they're going.

New York is alien to me, a visual experience so far removed from what I'm used to that it's hard to adjust. You have a nice meal in a restaurant with a white linen tablecloth and good silver, and a wino presses his nose and his bottle to the window and looks in at you, all his belongings in a plastic garbage bag he carries with him. People cuss and scream at each other from their cars, and nobody gives an inch. People sleep on the sidewalk, on benches, in doorways. Pedestrians step over them.

The people in this city don't seem to see things like that. They advise you to look the other way, to make no direct eye contact with anybody.

There are humans of every size and description and age and color walking the streets, an endless parade in a place that never sleeps, a place that holds many surprises. A crowd of people is gathered on a sidewalk watching a tall handsome young man with long flowing hair and no arms drawing a bright angel on the sidewalk with colored chalk he holds between his toes. The car horns blare, the traffic lights change, the finely dressed walk beside those whose clothes are shabby.

Out walking around and looking at the city, I'm coming close to a decision, one I've been thinking about for a long time. It's not an easy thing to decide, and there won't be any turning back. It will be like leaving a family I've had for nearly sixteen years. We work together and we play together, hunt, fish, go to the bars, hang out at the lake cooking fish and drinking beer from a keg. We help each other help people.

All that seems so far from here, but I know that in a few days I'll be back in the station, back on my streets, back behind the wheel of Engine 4 and Engine 10. This is only temporary, this will not last. But writing will last for the rest of my life.

I stand in my hotel room that evening before bed, looking out over Central Park. The sound of the traffic and the horns is always constant. I don't go to sleep easily once I lie down. There are too many things running through my mind.

I sit in the green room at NBC the next morning, having coffee. They've already had me in make-up, doing whatever they've done to me. I want a cigarette but I'm not allowed to smoke in here. I say hi to Surgeon General C. Everett Koop, but he only frowns when he sees the Marlboros in my pocket. Later, on the monitor, we watch him being interviewed. Then it's my turn.

Two nights later I'm tearing down a ceiling in Murphy's Marine, a bait shop/grocery store/gas station in Oxford, looking for pockets of fire. Our crew has knocked the fire down quickly but we're looking for embers, something still smoldering behind a wall or up in the ceiling. It's a rainy night and we have to climb up on the roof and lay out some vinyl salvage covers to keep the rain out until the morning, when repairs can begin.

The main thing everybody wants to know is if Jane Pauley is as good-looking in person as she is on television.

Yeah, she's a fox, I tell them. What I can't tell them is that appearing on that television show has changed something, the shape and order and regularity my world once had. People know where I am now, and they can call me when I'm on duty at the station. A man calls me up and tells me a long and awful story about being driven out of the U.S. Army, and wants me to write a movie or a book about it. A man calls me up and tells me a long and awful story about a land dispute he's involved in, which has caused the suicide of his sister. He wants me to write a book or a movie about it. A lawyer calls me up and tells me he has the most interesting case in the world, which would make a great movie or book. A woman calls me up and tells me that her life is a combination of *Silkwood* and one other movie, and wants, naturally, a book or a movie. Cranks, creeps, preachers, the desperately-wanting-to-publish. I can't hide from them anymore. If *Dirty Work* does even moderately well it will get worse instead of better.

There's enough money in my retirement fund to live on for a couple of years, probably. Even if I fail, even if I can't make a living from my books, even if I have to go back to driving a forklift or painting houses or sacking groceries in some store, at least I'll have those two years to try, to give it everything I've got, to take my chance at it.

It's a spring night in 1990, and my friend and I are driving leisurely down Old Highway 6, drinking a beer, heading out to my house for supper. We're talking, laughing, listening to music. The city gave me a nice retirement ceremony, took my badge and brass and one shoulder patch and mounted it all in a good glass case and handed me a special proclamation from the Mayor's office. They wanted me to say a few words, but I couldn't think of many to say. How do you say goodbye to a family?

The red lights come up behind us quickly, and I pull over to the side of the road. The red pickup shoots by, the crash truck right behind it, OFD written on their doors. I know there's a wreck they're going to, and I want to see where it is, see who's working it.

We pull out and follow them down the road, although

they quickly run off and leave us, but I figure we can find the wreck if we just keep going on Old 6.

It's miles and miles before we run up on it, probably six or seven miles past my house, but once we get near it and see all the cars parked up and down both sides of the road, there's no doubt that we've found it.

We park the car and get out and walk up to the scene of the wreck. The powerful halogen lights are set up, illuminating the car run head-on into a tree, the front end smashed and crumpled. The firefighters are down in the ditch with the car, the hum of the Hurst Tool running high in the night. The ambulance crew waits while the state troopers direct traffic. Probably a hundred people are watching the firefighters work. I think I recognize some of them under their turnouts and helmets: Johnny, Tony, Bill, Ed, Michael, Vern. They are concentrating on what they're doing, the luminous stripes on their turnouts glowing in the light. They are working together, freeing the person in the car. This brotherhood of men: this is what I gave up. This is what I left behind.

We're standing in a small group of spectators who are watching the rescue continue, but we must be too close. A highway cop comes up and impatiently orders all of us to move back, out of the way, and let the firefighters do their work.

I see how things are now. I step to the other side of the road.

I have left all that now forever, even though in my heart I am still one of them. The boys are still there in the station, their shining trucks parked at the ready, and when trouble comes they roll to meet it, screaming beneath the leaves of the big oaks that line and shade North Lamar.